# RELIGIOUS FAITH IN
# CORRECTIONAL CONTEXTS

# RELIGIOUS FAITH IN
# CORRECTIONAL CONTEXTS

## Kent R. Kerley

FIRST**FORUM**PRESS

A DIVISION OF LYNNE RIENNER PUBLISHERS, INC. • BOULDER & LONDON

Published in the United States of America in 2014 by
FirstForumPress
A division of Lynne Rienner Publishers, Inc.
1800 30th Street, Boulder, Colorado 80301
www.firstforumpress.com

and in the United Kingdom by
FirstForumPress
A division of Lynne Rienner Publishers, Inc.
3 Henrietta Street, Covent Garden, London WC2E 8LU

**Library of Congress Cataloging-in-Publication Data**
Kerley, Kent R.
Religious faith in correctional contexts / Kent R. Kerley.
Includes bibliographical references and index.
ISBN 978-1-935049-91-3 (hc: alk. paper)
1. Prisoners—Religious life. 2. Criminals—Rehabilitation. I. Title.
HV8865.K47 2013
204'.4086'9270973—dc23                                                  2013028309

**British Cataloguing in Publication Data**
A Cataloguing in Publication record for this book
is available from the British Library.

This book was produced from digital files prepared by the author
using the FirstForumComposer.

Printed and bound in the United States of America

⊗     The paper used in this publication meets the requirements
       of the American National Standard for Permanence of
       Paper for Printed Library Materials Z39.48-1992.

5  4  3  2  1

# Contents

# Acknowledgments

Many people contributed professionally to this research endeavor. Andrew Berzanskis of FirstForumPress first contacted me about doing this book and was a great encouragement during the process. Special thanks to my colleagues Heith Copes, John Sloan, Todd Matthews, and Troy Blanchard for helpful comments on drafts of several chapters. Most of all, thanks for your friendship.

Special thanks also to my top-notch research assistants at the University of Alabama at Birmingham (UAB), Stephanie (Swizzle) Cardwell and Lindsay (LL) Leban, for extensive proofreading, for locating resources, for making sure the manuscript format was consistent, and for vetting all of my hip cultural references. I thank three of my honors students, Jamie Bell, Steven Buckelew, and Kathryn Stahl Smith, for help in developing portions of Chapters 5 and 7. To be as inclusive as possible, I thank all of the faculty, staff, and students at UAB and Mississippi State University (MSU) who made some contribution to this work.

I want to thank the National Science Foundation for funding our summer Research Experiences for Undergraduates program (Award #1004953, 2010–2012). As a result of this great program, twelve talented students from across the nation contributed to this book: Lauren Eason, Alana Linn, Minh Nguyen, Ariana Stone, Candi Witzigreuter, Mercedez Dunn, Kuniko Madden, Maddy Semon, Lindsay Leban, Jess Deitzer, Leah Taylor, and Christine Agnone.

On a personal level I want to thank my best friend and spouse, Lori, for her unyielding support during my work on this project. While sitting in a pedal boat in the middle of the lake at Oak Mountain State Park, you helped me sketch an outline for this book over a year before the writing began in earnest. You are so awesome! Thanks also go to my 14-year-old Cockerpoo, Lexi, for being a calming influence snuggled up to my leg as I worked. Special thanks go to my parents for their generous love and support. Recently we have grown closer than ever, and I hope that you both will be proud of this work. Thanks go to my sister for sending me videos and photos of her two cool babies as they grow up.

Those were a lot of fun and a great stress reliever at times. Last but not least, thanks go to my two children and "Great Eight" grandchildren for making life so much fun. We have a framed art piece in our house that says it all: "A grandchild fills a space in your heart that you never knew was empty."

# 1

# The Faith of Captives

I spent the last decade going into prisons and halfway houses to study people who have committed all sorts of horrific crimes, mostly while under the influence of hard-core drugs—but now now claim to be "changed," "saved," or "born again." The underlying reason they cited for their dramatic change was a new or renewed religious faith. Let me share one striking example of this before-and-after scenario. I recall sitting in a damp, humid, and altogether depressing room where I interviewed an inmate assigned the name Klara. She recounted a difficult family life in which her mother spent time in several mental health institutions and, consequently, Klara "bounced back and forth" among several relatives. At one point she was even sent to foster care. She got into serious drug use in her early teens and continued using drugs even after having two children.

Klara was serving what may as well have been a life sentence for a long list of crimes. Chief among those was the attempted murder of a child: *her child*. Here she recounts what happened at the end of a week-long cocaine binge:

> My case is very difficult and everything. You know, I was hearing voices and hallucinations. I ended up taking a plea bargain of 25 years, but anyway, my daughter could've died. I thought I was saving her, and I put her in the oven.

It was all I could do as a researcher to digest what she just said in such a matter-of-fact manner and not give a negative verbal or nonverbal response. The same woman who so casually described placing her baby in a hot oven while high on cocaine was now an active participant in the prison's chapel services. She was even considered a spiritual mentor to other women in the prison. Here is how she described what had happened since she was incarcerated:

And I got baptized and everything, and I come back to the dorm, and it was like I had got drunk in the Holy Spirit. And I was so drunk coming back to the dorm. And I remember looking out the window, and there's just the most beautifulest rainbow out the window, you know, and it was just beautiful. And I couldn't make it a day in this prison without God. He's an awesome God. . . . And she lived [her baby], and she's this beautiful sweetheart today. And God is an awesome God. He let my daughter live. I hadn't seen my children in 7 years. And He just reunited me with my oldest daughter. I have two kids. He just reunited me with my oldest daughter and everything. She's forgiven me, and she understands. She was 7 at the time that it happened, and my baby was 14 months old.

How could this narrative of radical positive change belong to the same person who nearly killed her own baby? The only answer that Klara could provide was that a higher power had provided redemption.

If you watch television for a short while, soon you will see stories of homicide, rape, assault, child sexual abuse, drug addiction, and even terrorism. Not only are these crimes depicted in popular television shows and movies, but also real instances of them are depicted on local news networks, national news networks, 24-hour cable news networks, and online news sources. There is a rush among media commentators, political pundits, and even some academic researchers (assuming, of course, that media sources ask for our input) to explore the "criminal mind" of the accused. As details emerge in many criminal cases, we are told that the accused are evil and not likely to change.

But what if redemption, even for the worst offenders, is possible? What if people who commit vile acts can undergo radical change? If so, by what person or force can it happen? How does religious faith in prisons and halfway houses help offenders of all types to cope with the difficult institutional environment? What tools does faith provide for life after release from prisons and halfway houses?

### Genesis of the Project

To address these questions, let's go to the true beginning of this story. I flash back over ten years to a seemingly innocuous conversation with a neighbor. It was 2001, and during the span of six months I had accepted a job at Mississippi State University (MSU), completed my dissertation, got married, bought a house, and moved to Starkville, Mississippi. During my first semester as a new professor at MSU, a neighbor directly across the street came over to welcome my family to the neighborhood. He was a longtime professor at MSU in the School of Engineering and was very active in a local faith congregation. About five minutes into our conversation, he asked me a question central to the southern cultural experience: "Do you attend church?"

My response was that we had in the past, but we had not yet visited any churches in the area. He described his church and indicated that they would love for us to visit at some point. He went on to describe a national prison ministry program (Operation Starting Line) that was scheduled to visit the largest prison in Mississippi later that fall, as well as a weekly ministry he had established with inmates in the local jail. Initially I think his intent was to gauge my interest in volunteering to help with one of the ministry opportunities, yet my mind was focused on the possibilities for empirical research. Questions came to mind such as: "Who organizes and conducts these programs?" "What faith content is included?" and "What are the short- and long-term impacts of these programs?" We ended the conversation with a promise for my neighbor to send me an e-mail with more details about the programs with which he was involved.

Although I knew a great deal about prisons from my undergraduate and graduate coursework, as well as from writing my dissertation, I knew very little about the social scientific literature on religion. I fact, I had never even taken a course on religion. This was a bit intimidating, and yet I was excited about the prospects of studying faith-based prison programs. My major professor from graduate school, Dr. Mike Benson, always emphasized the need for me to work hard, to be opportunistic, and to establish a niche research area in the field. His wisdom made me think that this might be a great opportunity. I then did what any well-trained assistant professor should do and read everything I could find on religion in prison. Normally I would limit myself to articles in peer-reviewed journals and in scholarly books, but I wanted to be exhaustive in my reading on the topic. Unexpectedly, this searching and reading took only a few days as I only found a sparse amount of material. From my reading I reached several preliminary conclusions.

First, I noted that most of the literature on religion in prison appeared in non-peer-reviewed outlets and did not use strong social science methodologies. Some of the problems with those studies included small samples, nonrepresentative samples, and limited statistical analysis. Moreover, the majority of studies focused on whether faith-based prison programs could reduce the likelihood of rearrests (i.e., recidivism) among inmates after their release. This was not surprising given the emphasis on program evaluation in the field of criminal justice, but to me it seemed conceptually backward. How can we understand the effects of prison programs, especially ones that are faith-based, on inmates' attitudes and behaviors after prison if we do not first understand the impact on attitudes and behaviors while in prison?

Second, I noted the large number of studies conducted by the prison ministry providers themselves or commissioned by them. Not surprisingly, evaluations of various national, regional, and local prison programs were overwhelmingly positive and the programs promised even more sanguine results if only they could be expanded and receive greater funding. It was not uncommon to read of a program touting a recidivism rate of less than 40 percent (the national average is about 67 percent), and some claimed as little as 20 percent. I realized quickly that independent research with strong science methods was needed in the area.

Third, I noted that faith-based prison programs appeared to be a hot topic in national politics and according to most media sources. After assuming office in early 2001, President George Walker Bush, via Executive Order 13199, created the White House Office of Faith-Based and Community Initiatives (OFCBI). During the campaign, candidate Bush had been very public about his religious faith and in his support for faith-based programs of all stripes. It was no surprise, then, that he created an office that, among other things, would help local and state faith-based organizations that provide social services to compete for federal grants. This possibility existed because of the little-known "charitable choice" provision of the 1996 federal welfare bill. In addition to creation of the OFBCI, state departments of correction were engaged in debates over how best to rehabilitate inmates with as little funding as possible. Many states determined that faith-based prison programs had several advantages over many traditional correctional programs and thus began to use them more frequently.

Fourth, I noted a uniquely southern component to the literature on faith-based programs. Although the earliest use of faith-based prison programs was by the Quakers in the northeastern United States, in contemporary times prisons in the southern region appeared to use them more often and have more local faith congregations involved than any other part of the country. Moreover, rates of church attendance tend to be higher in the southern region than in other regions, and many scholars have written about the southern culture of religiosity (see, for example, Reed 1993). For all of those reasons, I am convinced that the South is the ideal research site for a study on faith-based prison programs.

I also want to comment in more detail on the political nature of the topic for this book. I learned quickly that there are often only two viewpoints on the utility and usefulness of religion as a method of correctional treatment or prison coping. On the one side, there are those who disagree with the concept of offering faith-based programs because of concerns about prisoner coercion. Groups such as Americans United for Separation of Church and State frequently have pursued legal action against states and programs that they feel create a coercive prison environment. At times they have adopted the position that faith-based programs should not be offered at all in prisons, with the rationale that requiring voluntary participation is too great a standard to achieve.

Even my colleagues in academia—those claiming to be scholars and not political activists—have shown significant bias at times. I once had a reviewer from *Justice Quarterly* (one of the top journals in criminology/criminal justice) who was "not comfortable with direct quotations from the Bible." You might be tempted to agree with the reviewer until you hear the full context. This was a paper on how inmates use faith to cope with incarceration and to create new prosocial identities while in prison. It involved an analysis of interviews with inmates who were actively involved in religious programs at a large prison in Mississippi. The inmates routinely paraphrased and referenced various Scriptures as they told their stories. To make these references clearer to readers, we looked up the handful of Scriptures most commonly referenced by the inmates and included those in the paper. That the reviewer had problems with scriptural references made by those being interviewed displayed a personal bias, and not a concern for strong social science standards.

On the other side are directors of national prison ministry programs and key leaders of evangelical Protestant congregations, especially in the southern region. For example, Charles Colson, former director of Prison Fellowship Ministries, was very visible in writing books and articles and conducting media interviews in support of faith-based programs. Unfortunately, this advocacy for faith-based prison programs has often led to the diminution and critique of all prison programs that are not faith-based, including many successful educational and vocational programs.

In some cases those who support the expansion of faith-based programs in prisons often neglect to think through the logistics of their programs, especially in terms of assuring that participation is voluntary and in specifying the role that prison chaplains and local congregants will play. I once had a chaplain tell me about a program where members of a local congregation came into a large unit that held about 150 inmates and held a weekly prayer and worship service. The program organizers claimed that the inmates had the choice of coming over to participate or not, but given the size of the unit and the loudness of the music and speakers, it was virtually impossible to document voluntary participation. One organizer allegedly told the chaplain that "we are okay with forcing some people to hear a little of our message since it is a good one." My view is that extreme positions on both sides of the issue have served to limit the creation of scientific knowledge.

Over the past decade I have collaborated with nearly two dozen faculty colleagues and students to study faith in correctional contexts. We have found positive, negative, and mixed results for the effects of faith-based programs in prisons, and my research has been criticized at times by both sides. Some have suggested that my results showing positive impacts of religion on prison coping are not as strong as I have portrayed them. Others have suggested that my results are too tempered, and that I should be more emphatic when my results are positive for religion. To be honest, I feel some degree of satisfaction from this and have concluded that it must be an indication that I have found a reasonable balance between two extreme positions. For me the main goal is to conduct studies that have strong social scientific standards. Whether analyzing survey data or interview transcripts, I do not pray or cross my fingers in hope of a particular result. My collaborators and I simply analyze the data and report the results. That may be difficult for ideologues and activists on both sides to understand, but it is the cornerstone of good science. In reading this book my hope is not that you will take a dogmatic position on the value of religion in correctional contexts, but simply that you will learn a great deal about the topic from an independent researcher.

## Summary and Plan for the Book

An impressive research literature has identified a significant relationship between religion and a wide range of attitudes, behaviors, and life events. Studies of the relationship between religion and crime or deviance in the general public and in prison have not always produced significant or uniform effects. Chapter 2 provides a review of the literature on religion and the commission of criminal and deviant acts, as well as the literature on the effects of religion on prison misconduct and recidivism. Chapter 3 explores the narratives of 30 chaplains and local religious congregants who organize and provide faith-based prison programs in Mississippi.

Chapter 4 describes the conversion experience from the research literature and then focuses on an analysis of the conversion narratives of 173 prisoners from Alabama and Mississippi. Chapter 5 details the lived experience of faith from the perspective of 63 incarcerated men at the Mississippi State Penitentiary in Parchman, Mississippi. Chapter 6 details the lived experience of faith from the perspective of 40 incarcerated women at the Janet Tutwiler Prison for Women in Wetumpka, Alabama.

Chapter 7 explores the narratives of 70 residents of a faith-based halfway house for women in Birmingham, Alabama. Chapter 8 explores the narratives of what 173 religious converts expect after release from prisons and halfway houses and how they claim faith will help them adjust to society and be successful. In the final chapter, Chapter 9, I bring together all of the scholarly concepts and findings from this work. I also focus on the future of faith-based programs, especially faith-based prison programs, from the vantage point of researchers, practitioners, and policymakers.

The purpose of this book is to understand the lived experience of religious faith in correctional contexts. In particular, I explore how individuals use faith to adapt and survive in difficult institutional settings such as prisons and halfway houses. I explore these topics via an analysis of 203 in-depth interviews. This total number was comprised of 103 inmates, 30 prison ministry workers, and 70 residents of a faith-based halfway house (see the Appendix for complete information on all data sources).

# 2

# The Relationship Between Religion and Criminal Behavior

The study of religion as an academic discipline is a fairly recent development in colleges and universities in the United States. Since the 1960s, researchers from social science backgrounds (mostly from sociology programs) have studied religion as a social force that may impact a wide range of individual and societal outcomes. In addition to the scholarly books and articles produced, evidence of interest in the sociology of religion includes the creation of multiple specialty journals, such as *Journal for the Scientific Study of Religion, Religions,* and *Review of Religious Research*. Likewise, the journals *Social Forces* and *Sociological Spectrum* have produced special issues on the sociology of religion in just the past five years.

This research stream has incorporated diverse research methodologies such as surveys, in-depth interviews, participant observation, and content analysis. The consistent finding is that religiosity—a cognitive and behavioral commitment to organized religion—may operate as a social force for increasing positive behaviors among those in the general public. Most studies suggest that religiosity is associated with prosocial outcomes such as interpersonal friendliness, psychological and physical well-being, comfort and coping in difficult life situations, martial happiness, participation in politics and political movements, and volunteering in community organizations (Ellison 1991, 1992; Ellison et al. 2001; Ellison and Levin 1998; Krause et al. 2001; Levin and Chatters 1998; Williams and Alexander 1994; Wilson and Musick 1997).

Many researchers have speculated on how religion may be linked to prosocial behaviors. Ellison (1992) provides perhaps the most cogent explanations. He explains the nexus in two ways. First, individuals with higher levels of religious commitment are more likely to engage in religious role taking such that they interact with others according to their perceptions of what a "divine other" would expect. The notion is that people of faith may view life "from the vantage point of the 'God-role,' by attempting to understand how a divine other would expect them to behave toward their fellows" (Ellison 1992, p. 413). Second, people of faith may internalize religious norms concerning kindness, empathy, and civility. Scriptural stories and precepts, such as "The Good Samaritan" and the Golden Rule, provide structure and a model for relationships with others.

Although the relationship between religion and prosocial behaviors appears relatively straightforward, the relationship between religion and antisocial behaviors is a bit more complicated (Kerley 2009). Before discussing this research, the important question to ask first is *how* religion might reduce criminal or deviant behaviors. The answer can be drawn from social capital (Coleman 1988) and social control theories (Hirschi 1969). Many researchers contend that religious involvement creates social networks and emotional support that may constrain criminal behavior. Religious individuals tend to be bonded to religious institutions that provide informal social control over their behaviors. The behavior of individuals with high levels of religiosity is thought to be constrained by the sanctions derived from religious thought. According to this logic, religiosity may operate as a shield against negative behaviors by creating and reinforcing social networks and social bonds.

The first major study of religion and crime was conducted by Hirschi and Stark (1969). The authors used survey data on California youths to test the Hellfire Hypothesis, which predicted that religion could deter crime among individuals through the fear of supernatural sanctions and could also encourage prosocial behaviors through the hope and promise of supernatural rewards. The point was to investigate whether individuals who attend church were less likely than individuals who do not attend church to engage in a variety of delinquent behaviors. They also investigated whether belief in supernatural sanctions for bad behavior served as a deterrent. They found no relationship between religious attendance or belief in supernatural sanctions and self-reported delinquent acts. The researchers concluded that the youths' decisions to commit crimes were linked with perceptions of pleasure and pain on earth, rather than perceived heavenly rewards for good behavior or hellfire for bad behavior. Since Hirschi and Stark's (1969) landmark study, investigators have produced about two major studies per year on this topic. Next I will review several of the key studies, which are arranged by the results.

**Positive Results**

Over a decade after the classic Hirschi and Stark (1969) paper was published, Stark, Kent, and Doyle (1982) came to the conclusion that findings from their original study were due largely to the moral makeup of Richmond, California, where the data were collected. In what became known as the Moral Communities Hypothesis, Stark and colleagues contended that religion is best understood as a structural property of communities rather than as an individual attribute of persons. In other words, religion is most likely to reduce crime and deviance in more religious regions of the country (e.g., Midwest, Southeast), and is less likely to do so in less religious regions (e.g., Northeast, Pacific Northwest). In terms of church membership and church attendance, Richmond, California, had very low rates of religious commitment compared to the rest of the country. Stark and colleagues characterized this area as a "secular community," as opposed to a "moral community."

Higgins and Albrecht (1977) also suggested that the failure to find a significant relationship between religiosity and delinquency in Hirschi and Stark's (1969) landmark study stemmed from the use of a sample from a primarily nonreligious Western population. They analyzed a sample drawn from the more religious-oriented South and found that religiosity led to reductions in self-reported crime and deviance. They also found that in addition to religiosity, peer expectations and relationships with parents were predictors of crime and deviance. Thus, Higgins and Albrecht concluded that Hirschi and Stark (1969) may have obtained accurate results for the western area they studied, but for studies in areas of the country characterized by strong religious communities, the results are likely to be the opposite.

Johnson and his colleagues (2001) analyzed data from the National Youth Survey and came to a slightly different conclusion about the relationship between religiosity and delinquency. The investigators attempted to explain involvement in 35 different types of delinquent behavior. In particular they focused on measures of religiosity, social control, and social learning. They found that religiosity directly reduced delinquent behavior, even after controlling for geographic region, youths' social bonds to society, and the extent of their delinquent associations. Welch, Tittle, and Grasmick (2006) examined the relationships among religiosity, self-control, and crime. They analyzed survey data on adults in Oklahoma to determine the key predictors of five different types of crimes. The authors found that religiosity and self-control operate on significant, independent tracks for deterring crime. In other words, higher levels of religious commitment directly reduced the likelihood of criminal activity even after controlling for individuals' level of self-control.

Spivak and colleagues (2011) examined the influence of religiosity and deterrence on crime and deviance among students at a large state university. The investigators conducted telephone surveys with a random sample of undergraduate students about the likelihood of engaging in various violations of the school's alcohol policy. To test the deterrent impact of informal sanctions, the authors asked questions about the degree of shame and embarrassment students would feel if they violated the alcohol policy. To measure religiosity, students were asked questions relating to religious salience, literal interpretations of Scriptures, and sinfulness. Religiosity was found to reduce the likelihood of anticipated violations of the alcohol policy. It also increased the perceived threats of shame and embarrassment for violations of the policy. These findings suggest that religiosity may reduce crime and deviance via an increased concern for the informal sanctions associated with deviant behaviors.

Of final note are multiple systematic reviews of the empirical literature on religion and many deleterious outcomes such as crime, delinquency, and deviance. Johnson and colleagues (Johnson, Larson, et al. 2000) reviewed 40 studies of the relationship between religion and delinquency conducted between 1985 and 1997. They found that in 30 of them religion led to significant reductions. Baier and Wright (2001) reviewed 60 studies of religion and crime and deviance conducted between 1969 and 1998. They concluded that, overall, religion had a "moderate" inverse effect on crime and deviance. The most recent and most comprehensive review of the literature appears in Johnson's (2011) recent book, *More God, Less Crime: Why Faith Matters and How It Could Matter More*. In this work he reviewed 272 studies conducted between 1944 and 2010. He found that in 90 percent of the studies, the authors reported an "inverse or beneficial relationship between religion and some measure of crime or delinquency" (Johnson 2011, p. 78; see also Johnson and Jang 2012). Here is Johnson's cogent summary of his findings:

Until recently there has been a lack of consensus about the nature of this relationship between religion and crime. Based on our exhaustive review of the studies utilizing vastly different methods, samples, and research designs, increasing religiosity is consistently linked with decreases in various measures of crime or delinquency. As expected, these findings are particularly pronounced among the more methodologically and statistically sophisticated studies, especially those relying upon nationally representative samples. Put simply, we find increasing religiousness to be associated with decreases in crime or delinquency. The weight of this evidence is especially intriguing in light of the fact that so many researchers continue to overlook religion (Johnson 2011, p. 79).

## Negative or Mixed Results

Other investigators have found either no relationship between religion and crime, only a partial relationship, or in some cases a spurious relationship. Burkett and White (1974) offered an interesting explanation for findings from the Hirschi and Stark (1969) study. They suggested that the effects of religion on crime will vary depending on the type of crime. Using survey data on high school students in Pennsylvania, they found that religion is most likely to reduce behaviors that have a strong moral connotation in religious circles, but are not universally looked down upon in society (e.g., alcohol and drug use, gambling, premarital sex). The authors reported that higher levels of religious participation led to significant decreases in students' use of alcohol and marijuana, but it did not impact involvement in property or violent offenses. This finding serves as the basis for what is called the Antiasceticism Hypothesis.

Using data on middle and high school students in three Midwest states, Cochran and Akers (1989) reached a similar conclusion to that of Burkett and White (1974). The authors tested several theories of the relationship between crime and delinquency, and found that the Antiasceticism Hypothesis received the most support. The more religious students in the sample reported significantly lower levels of alcohol and marijuana use than less religious or nonreligious students, but there was no significant effect of religion on other types of crimes.

Ellis (1987) has suggested that the relationship between religion and crime is spurious. That is, the relationship is contingent upon another factor, which is the arousal level of each individual. According to Arousal Theory, criminal behavior is related to innate variations in each individual's demand for neurological stimulation. Ellis argues that criminals are naturally prone to boredom and that criminal actions are a means of finding arousal through risk-seeking behavior. When individuals have suboptimal arousal levels (the tendency to be bored), they will seek stimulation to meet their psychological and physiological needs. It is not that all stimulation sought by these individuals will be criminal, but that the risk-seeking behaviors may, in some cases, be criminal. In terms of religiosity, Ellis predicts that individuals who have suboptimal arousal levels will have low levels of church attendance, since religious services often are routine and solemn events. In a test of his theory, Ellis (1987) measured religion based on church membership, church attendance, belief in God, denominational measures, belief in immortality, and other beliefs. He then measured arousal in two ways: neurological and extraneurological. The neurological measure included basic brain wave readings measured with electroencephalography (EEG). Extraneurological measures were divided into two subcategories: physiological and self-reported measures. Physiological measures involved skin conductivity and other arousal indicators such as heart and pulse rates, startle reflexes, and adrenaline secretions. The self-reported measures consisted of responses about the exciting and boring activities in which participants regularly engaged.

Ellis (1987) summarized three findings from this study: (1) among church members, those who attended church more often exhibited lower crime rates than those whose attendance was infrequent, (2) those who believed in an afterlife where their sins would be punished had lower crime rates than those who lacked the same belief, and (3) Jewish crime rates were lower than for Christians, and Protestants had lower crime rates than Catholics. He concluded that religious participation was associated with lower levels of criminal conduct. However, he found that the relationship between religion and crime was not strong once the level of arousal was added to the analysis. Thus, Ellis concluded that arousal level was the best predictor of both religiosity and criminal behavior.

Cochran, Wood, and Arneklev (1994) used data on high school students in Oklahoma to investigate whether religion could reduce the incidence of several different types of crimes. Along with measures of religiosity, the authors included measures from Arousal and Social Control Theories. Similar to Ellis (1987), the authors found that the relationship between religion and crime was spurious. More specifically, it disappeared once the arousal levels and social controls of the individuals were considered. Benda and Corwyn (1997) analyzed data on students in three Arkansas high schools to determine whether religion was related to several different types of delinquent and criminal behaviors. They found that greater levels of religiosity (church attendance, in particular) reduced the likelihood of status offenses (e.g., skipping school, giving fake excuses for missing school, and running away), but did not reduce the likelihood of crimes against persons or property. When the measures of social control were added, however, the relationship between religiosity and status offenses disappeared and there was still no effect of religiosity on crime.

Most recently, Ulmer and colleagues (2012) studied religion and just one type of crime. The investigators used data from the National Longitudinal Study of Adolescent Health (Add Health) to examine the relationship between adolescent religious involvement and use of marijuana. They used a life-course approach in which they examined the religion-marijuana relationship in terms of initiation, persistence, and desistance. They also found that adolescent religious involvement had a preventative effect on initiation into marijuana use, but did not explain persistence and desistance.

## Religion in Prison

Religion has been a tool for correctional treatment since the inception of the penal system in the United States. In fact, the first penitentiaries were developed by Quakers as places where offenders could study the Bible as part of their rehabilitation. National prison ministry organizations, such as Bill Glass's Champions for Life and Charles Colson's Prison Fellowship Ministries, have worked in US prisons since the 1970s. Most states currently employ full-time chaplains and allow members of local religious congregations to conduct services in their prison facilities. The focus in most prisons is not simply on the provision of religious services, but also on the daily practice of faith.

Religion in prison thus is not some new concept or policy directive. What is new, however, is the context in which faith-based prison programs have been developed, refined, and studied. To tell this story fully, some background statistics are needed. The criminal justice system in the United States has experienced unprecedented growth over the past four decades. According to a Bureau of Justice Statistics report from 2012 (BJS 2012a), since 1980 the total prison population has expanded from about 330,000 inmates to just under 1.6 million inmates. As I write this book, I note something rather remarkable. For the year 2011, the total prison population *decreased* for only the second time since 1972. Four decades of what Austin and Irwin (2012) have dubbed the "imprisonment binge" have certainly impacted the nation. The imprisonment rate for 2011 is still an alarming 497 per 100,000 residents, which means that about 1 in every 200 residents is behind bars (BJS 2012). One of every 34 adults living in the United States in 2011 was under some type of correctional authority, such as jail, prison, probation, or parole (BJS 2012). Given these numbers, it should come as no surprise that the criminal justice system has been the fastest-growing segment of spending in many states, even surpassing spending on education. Despite the vast investment of resources devoted to crime control, large-scale imprisonment has produced only minor impacts on the goals of dramatically reducing crime and victimization rates, making people feel safer, and deterring offenders from committing other crimes. According to a landmark report by the Bureau of Justice Statistics (BJS 2002), nearly 68 percent of inmates in the United States who were released in 1994 were rearrested within three years. The idea of a "revolving door" in prisons appears to be an empirical reality.

Considering the numbers of individuals imprisoned, there seems a clear need for effective correctional treatment. Programs that have shown promise focus on literacy, General Educational Development (GED, equivalent to a high school diploma), and college training, work and life skills training, and substance abuse treatment (Andrews et al. 1990; Cullen and Gendreau 2001; Gendreau and Little 1996; Gibbons 1999; Lipton 1996). Unfortunately, these programs typically are expensive. Given limited operating budgets, most states spend as little as possible on correctional treatment. Moreover, in many states there is active political pressure to reduce spending for correctional treatment.

This is where religion enters. In addition to concerns about correctional spending, two key things happened since the mid-1990s that signaled a renewed interest in religion and faith-based prison programs. First was passage of the "charitable choice" provision of the 1996 welfare bill, which allows faith-based organizations that provide social services to compete for federal grants. Second, after assuming office in early 2001, President George Walker Bush, via Executive Order 13199, created the White House Office of Faith-Based and Community Initiatives (OFCBI). During his campaign, President Bush had been very public about his religious faith and in his support for faith-based programs of all stripes. It was no surprise, then, that he created an office that, among other things, would help local and state faith-based organizations that provide social services to compete for federal grants. Although the OFCBI has been renamed and restructured under the Barack Obama administration, faith-based programs remain a priority.

The important question for us now is whether and how religiosity and faith-based programs can be effective in improving the lives of inmates while in prison and, by extension, once they are released. Academic research on this issue is still relatively small, but a growing number of academic articles and even an edited collection (O'Connor and Pallone 2002) have been published in the past two decades. Researchers studying religion in prison have focused on two issues: (1) whether inmates' level of religiosity impacts prison behavior and (2) whether religiosity reduces the likelihood of arrest after release (i.e., recidivism).

One of the first studies in this area was conducted by Clear and his colleagues (1992). The researchers did not study the impact of faith-based prison programs, but rather studied whether individual religiosity—derived from any source before or after incarceration—affected prison adjustment and prison infractions. Using a nonrandom sample of 769 inmates located at twenty different US prisons, Clear et al. (1992) found that inmate religiosity significantly increased inmates' ability to cope with incarceration and significantly decreased their level of prison infractions. Clear and Sumter (2002) reached the same conclusion.

Johnson (1987b) studied 782 inmates released from a Florida prison between 1978 and 1982, and found that religious conversion in prison was not a significant predictor of subsequent attendance at prison religious services, post-release religiosity, or post-release church attendance. In a separate study using the same dataset, Johnson (1987a) found that inmates' religiosity, chaplains' assessment of inmate religiosity, and inmates' religious service attendance did not affect the number of prison infractions committed or the amount of time spent in disciplinary confinement. Johnson (1987a, p. 24) concluded that "while religion may inhibit deviance for the general population, it does not inhibit rule violating behavior among a certain segment of that population."

A decade later, Johnson, Larson, and Pitts (1997) conducted an evaluation of a faith-based program sponsored by Prison Fellowship Ministries (PFM). A sample of prisoners in four New York state prisons was chosen because PFM staff kept thorough records in those facilities. Among the 40,000 inmates in the four prisons, 201 male prisoners were chosen based on their similarities to the control group. Inmates were categorized based on their participation in three different religious programs and the length of time they were involved. Inmates who participated in 10 or more activities per year were considered "highly active," those participating in 1 to 9 programs were considered "medium active," and those who did not attend any were classified as "inactive." They evaluated inmates' incident records while incarcerated as well as their arrest records for one year after release. They found that participation in PFM activities was not related to prison infractions. In fact, inmates who were most active in PFM activities were most likely to have a record of serious prison infractions. The researchers were unable to determine which activity came first (the PFM activity or the infraction), but suggested that the inmates might have committed the infractions and then turned to religion to make amends. Inmates involved in PFM activities did not have a significantly reduced likelihood of recidivism compared to the control group. However, Johnson et al. (1997) found that inmates in the "highly active" group were much less likely to have been arrested one year after their release than individuals in the control group.

In 2004, Johnson conducted a follow-up study with several important modifications. First, he lowered the number of activities in which inmates must participate to be considered having high participation from 10 or greater to 5 or greater. Second, he had eight years of tracking data on inmates. Johnson (2004) found little difference between the median arrest times and reincarceration rates of PFM and non-PFM inmates. The "survival rate" (the rate at which they were arrested after release) was slightly lower for the PFM group after eight years, but the only significant differences appeared when high-participation inmates were compared to low-participation inmates. Overall, PFM program attendance was not a significant predictor of recidivism once all factors were considered. Johnson concluded that there was little difference in recidivism rates between inmates at different levels of participation even after eight years.

Clear and colleagues (2000) studied the potential benefits of any type of faith-based prison activity. They noted that while religion may be popular as a way to reduce recidivism, historically, any method for reducing recidivism will fall out of favor if it does not produce significant results. They sought to determine what benefits inmates could receive from religious activities in prisons. Clear et al. (2000) used both survey and ethnographic data on inmates involved in Christian and Muslim religious activities over the course of ten months. They examined the intrinsic value of being outwardly religious for prisoners, which they defined as the part that religion plays in helping them deal with the negative feelings they experienced due to their incarceration. The results indicated that inmates who were active in religious activities differed from those who were not active in regard to emotional health, prosocial behaviors, and the benefits they received. They found that faith allowed inmates to receive forgiveness and to make restitution for their offenses. Also, it gave them hope that they could turn their lives around when they were released. The most religiously active inmates reported that religion allowed them a mental escape from the realities of prison life and helped to prevent involvement in activities that could cause them trouble.

The authors also examined the extrinsic values of religious participation in terms of how faith affects inmates' relationships with others. Involvement in religious activities benefited inmates by providing them with a safe context in which to forge positive relationships in prison. These friends ensured a measure of safety. Especially for inmates practicing Islam, being part of a group provided them with a certain amount of protection, because their group was obligated to protect them. Additionally, the physical act of going to religious activities or acting out religious rituals kept inmates out of trouble and in safe places such as the chapel. Being active in religious programs also allowed inmates to create relationships with individuals visiting from outside. This contact with those in the free world gave inmates a feeling that they had not been forgotten by society. The authors concluded that religious activities in prison can provide inmates with a way of coping with the shock that prison life can present (Clear et al. 1992; Clear and Sumter 2002).

Kerley, Matthews, and Blanchard (2005) studied the effect of religiosity on negative prison behaviors, such as arguments and fights. A random sample of inmates at a large southeastern prison facility completed a survey relating to personal background, religious background, involvement in religious activities, and fighting or arguing with other inmates. The key outcome measures were arguing with other inmates and fighting with other inmates one or more times per month. The authors found a significant correlation between religiosity and the amount of arguments in which inmates engaged. Inmates who reported a belief in a higher power, regularly attended religious services, or attended Operation Starting Line (a special event sponsored by Prison Fellowship Ministries) were only half as likely to get into arguments with other inmates than those in the reference groups. Belief in a higher power reduced the likelihood of inmates getting into frequent arguments by over 70 percent. Even with controls for demographic factors and criminal history, religiosity (in both its cognitive and behavioral dimensions) appeared to be related directly to the likelihood of inmate arguments. Religiosity did not directly reduce inmate fighting, but did so indirectly by reducing the frequency of arguments. Given that physical conflicts in prison (as in the general public) generally result from the escalation of verbal conflicts, the connection seems clear. The authors concluded that religiosity may reduce the likelihood of fighting by reducing the odds that inmates will get into arguments.

In a follow-up study, Kerley, Allison, and Graham (2006) focused on whether religiosity and religious participation could help individuals cope with the uniquely stressful life event of being incarcerated. The survey asked inmates to report how often they experienced six different negative emotions: sadness, worry, anger, stress, depression, and bitterness. The researchers found that religiosity did not lead to a significant reduction in the experience of those negative emotions. They concluded that prisons are dehumanizing in the sense that they strip individuals of freedom, dignity, and identity. Thus, prison life may be emotionally debilitating to the point that religiosity does not reduce the experience of negative emotions.

I noted previously that some studies of religion and crime in the general public have found that the relationship is spurious. In short, another factor—such as self-control, social control, impulsivity, or arousal –may explain both religiosity and the commission of criminal and deviant behaviors. Drawing from these findings, one recent study was the first to examine this topic in the prison context. Kerley et al. (2011) used data on Iowa parolees to conduct the first investigation of religiosity, self-control, and deviant behavior in prison. The authors analyzed survey data from a sample of 208 recently paroled male inmates in Iowa. Their results indicated declining statistical significance as they tracked the impact of religiosity on prison deviance across their models. By themselves, all three measures of religiosity were significant predictors of prison deviance, but when measures of criminal history and demographic background were added, only two measures were significant. Once the authors accounted for the level of self-control, only one measure of religiosity (frequency of attending religious services) was significant. This led the authors to conclude that the relationship between religiosity and prison deviance was moderated partially by self-control. Stated another way, both religiosity and self-control were important theoretical constructs in explaining prison deviance.

Camp et al. (2006) collected survey data from 407 inmates participating in the faith-based Life Connections Program (LCP) at five treatment prisons and 592 comparison subjects at five other prisons (total N = 999). The authors found that inmates who participate in religious programs are "seeking their way" in a religious sense. They found that inmates who had a religious identity prior to incarceration were less likely to volunteer for religious programs offered in prison. They concluded that religious programs are effective in reducing prison deviance and recidivism only for those inmates who are highly involved, and not for inmates who have only a moderate or small amount of involvement. In a follow-up study that included survey data and official prison records, Camp et al. (2008) investigated whether involvement in the faith-based LCP reduced the likelihood of prison misconduct. They found that LCP participation decreased the probability of inmates engaging in serious forms of misconduct. However, there was no effect of LCP participation on less serious forms of misconduct or on both types of misconduct committed at the same time.

# 3

# Faith-Based Prison Programs and Prison Ministry Workers

When considering the lived experience of faith in correctional contexts, the tendency is to think only in terms of prison inmates who practice their faith while incarcerated. One important group that is often overlooked is the prison ministry workers who create an environment conducive to the practice of faith. Unfortunately, little rigorous research has been conducted on prison ministry workers and their provision of programs, and the bulk of prior studies has relied on survey data. Qualitative methodologies may be more ideally suited for describing the contours of prison ministry work. In this chapter I explore the narratives of these important, yet understudied, religious adherents. Specifically, I examine the narratives of 30 active prison chaplains and local religious congregants from the Mississippi Delta region. Before describing the rich themes from this analysis, some background information from the research literature on prison ministry workers is needed.

## Prison Chaplains

Prison chaplains are one of the few potentially humanizing elements in prisons. Chaplains have been used extensively in prisons since their creation. In fact, the first penitentiaries in the United States were developed by Quakers for offenders to study the Bible as part of their rehabilitation. The research literature on chaplains is fairly underdeveloped. Perhaps the most common topic in the literature is the historical transformation of chaplains' duties from guiding inmates to spiritual conversion to serving as counselors, organizers, and liaisons for inmates (Glaser 1964; Heiney, McWayne, and Teas 2007). One particular concern for chaplains is balancing the provision of religious programs with active proselytization of inmates. The long-accepted practice of using inmates as a "captive audience" for chaplains to proselytize has been largely abandoned (Acorn 1990; Heiney, McWayne, and Teas 2007; Sundt and Cullen 1998, 2002). It is unethical, and in most cases illegal, for chaplains to force inmates to attend religious services. In addition to not forcing their beliefs on inmates, prison chaplains must be respectful of whatever religious beliefs are present in the prison. While the majority of inmates and chaplains identify with some form of Christianity, a growing minority adhere to other faith traditions such as Islam, Buddhism, and Judaism. Contemporary chaplains must ensure that inmates have the materials necessary to fulfill the religious rites of the faith tradition to which they adhere.

Sundt and Cullen (1998) conducted the first major study of prison chaplains. The authors mailed surveys to a national sample of chaplains and received 232 completed questionnaires. They hypothesized that chaplains would see spiritual duties as their primary responsibility, but would report spending more time on secular duties. The authors found that chaplains consider the secular activity of counseling inmates to be their highest priority and the thing on which they spend the most time. The study showed that with the exception of the time spent coordinating volunteers, chaplains mostly spent their time on the tasks they perceived to be most important. Most chaplains perceived their role to be primarily supportive of inmates, but custodial activities were a substantial part of their job as well.

The survey also measured chaplains' support for treatment, the amount of counseling done by chaplains, and the content of the counseling sessions. Most chaplains favored treatment and rehabilitation, along with punishment, and did not see the rehabilitation model as a failure. They found that chaplains used a variety of counseling methods during their sessions; however, most reported using a spiritual orientation (Sundt, Dammer, and Cullen 2002).

Finally, the survey was used to determine chaplains' perspectives on the purpose of imprisonment. Sundt and Cullen (2002) found that almost half of the chaplains thought that the primary purpose of incarceration should be incapacitation. When forced to choose between rehabilitation and punishment, however, a clear majority of the chaplains chose rehabilitation. Not surprisingly, chaplains thought that religion was the best method for rehabilitating inmates. The authors concluded that chaplains support rehabilitation and consider their work to be such. Chaplains who felt called to work in chaplaincy and those who viewed God as forgiving were most likely to have a rehabilitative view of offenders.

## Local Religious Congregants

As the responsibilities of prison chaplains change and prison populations increase, local religious congregants have become a more integral part of faith-based prison programs. With an increase in secular responsibilities and budget deficits in prisons across the nation, chaplains increasingly rely on local religious congregants to create an environment where inmates can seek and experience religious faith. Local religious congregants can be especially helpful when inmates have spiritual requests for which chaplains are not trained or equipped to respond. Tewksbury and Dabney (2004) found that nearly 60 percent of prison volunteers reported contributing financial or material goods to their work. That amounts to substantial support in overcrowded prison systems where budgets for rehabilitation programs are scarce. The downside, of course, in looking to the community members for help is that as a result of budget cuts and political considerations, chaplains are being replaced by local religious congregants to cut costs. This can be problematic when local religious congregants do not have proper training to work in prisons.

Tewksbury and his colleagues conducted two studies of prison volunteers. In the first study, Tewksbury and Dabney (2004) surveyed volunteers at a southern prison who attended a mandatory training session. The point of the survey was to determine who volunteered, why they volunteered, and how they benefited from the experience. The most often reported motivation for going into prisons was to share religious beliefs. Other reasons for volunteering were to help others, because they were asked to do so, and because they had a relative in prison.

In a more recent study, Tewksbury and Collins (2005) surveyed a group of local religious congregants involved in faith-based prison work in three Kentucky prisons to learn more about the motivations and perceived rewards from the work. The vast majority identified with some form of Christianity, and most had served more than one but less than ten years as a volunteer. Their most commonly reported tasks were teaching, preaching, counseling, and studying religious texts. Nearly all prison volunteers reported intrinsic rewards such as feeling that they were serving God and had a true sense of purpose.

These previous studies have provided solid survey-based information about prison ministry workers. In my view the clear need is for in-depth qualitative inquiries of these workers. In what follows I explore the narratives of chaplains and local religious congregants from the Mississippi Delta region. All 30 interviewees were involved in part-time or full-time ministry work at one or more prisons at the time of the interview (see Appendix for detailed study methodology). Three key questions will be addressed in this chapter: (1) Who are these people? (2) What are their motivations? (3) What are their goals and expectations?

## Prison Ministry Workers: Who Are These People?

Table 3.1 provides a snapshot of the 30 prison ministry workers in the study. These chaplains and local congregants were very similar in terms of demographic characteristics such as age, race, gender, level of educational attainment, and socioeconomic status. Many of the chaplains and local congregants had been or were currently ministers at the churches they attended, which made it impossible to distinguish between the two groups. There was also overlap in that several of the prison chaplains also did volunteer work in prison facilities other than those in which they were employed, and some local congregants previously had worked in prisons as chaplains or as correctional officers. The chaplains varied in terms of whether they were full-time, paid employees and or were under contract as unpaid volunteers. Thus, given the similarities, I treat the 30 interview subjects as one relatively homogenous group of conservative Protestant prison ministry workers (Kerley et al. 2010; Kerley, Matthews, and Shoemaker 2009).

In terms of demographic characteristics for the interviewees, the average age was 47, with all respondents between the ages of 35 and 65. Eleven of the respondents were black and 19 were white. Five were women and 25 were men. In terms of educational attainment and socioeconomic status, the group average was a four-year college degree and the majority could be described as middle class or lower middle class. The results for income are particularly striking, especially given the educational status of the ministry workers. Twenty-four of the workers had a baccalaureate degree or higher, and yet only 10 had an income of $40,000 or higher. Only 2 of the 10 individuals in this top income category were prison chaplains, and they had income from other sources.

In Mississippi, as in most states, chaplains tend to be well-educated yet do not receive commensurate financial compensation Their workweeks typically far exceed 40 hours, and they face many formal and informal obstacles in their attempts to become agents of change in the prison context (Glaser 1964). One chaplain with a postgraduate degree described the financial compensation for chaplains as "miserly," and yet reported a high degree of job satisfaction and contentment:

**Table 3.1. Selected Characteristics of Interviewees (N = 30)**

|  | Percentage |
|---|---|
| Type of Prison Ministry Work |  |
| Full-time chaplains (paid) | 36.67 (N = 11) |
| Part-time chaplains (paid) | 10.00 (N = 3) |
| Contract chaplains (unpaid) | 6.67 (N = 2) |
| Local congregants (unpaid) | 46.66 (N = 14) |
| Age (median) | 47.50 years |
| Race |  |
| Black | 36.67 (N = 11) |
| White | 63.33 (N = 19) |
| Gender |  |
| Men | 83.33 (N = 25) |
| Women | 16.67 (N = 5) |
| Education |  |
| Some graduate school or advanced degree | 23.33 (N = 7) |
| Four-year college degree | 56.67 (N = 17) |
| High school degree and some college | 20.00 (N = 6) |
| Income |  |
| $40,000 and above | 33.33 (N = 10) |
| $25,000–$39,999 | 46.67 (N = 14) |
| $0–$24,999 | 20.00 (N = 6) |
| Religious Affiliation |  |
| African Methodist Episcopal (AME) Zion | 10.00 (N = 3) |
| Baptist | 30.00 (N = 9) |
| Church of Christ | 23.34 (N = 7) |
| Church of God | 13.33 (N = 4) |
| Methodist | 13.33 (N = 4) |
| Presbyterian | 10.00 (N = 3) |

No matter the money, I try as best as I can not to be in a hurry becauseone thing that I have come to understand is that listening is probably one of the greatest parts of ministry here at the prison. There's just something about being there and lending an ear, that seems to really have a profound effect upon the offender. I guess it's them feeling accepted, that they matter, and that their words matter.

The chaplains believed that the intrinsic value of prison ministry work outweighed any extrinsic deficits.

In terms of religious affiliation, all study participants were involved actively in a local religious congregation. The majority of their congregations could be characterized as theologically conservative, evangelical, and Protestant, with most reporting membership in African Methodist Episcopal (AME) Zion, Baptist, Church of Christ, Church of God, Methodist, or Presbyterian churches. Although these denominations vary in theology, culture, political orientation, and worship style in different regions of the country, in rural Mississippi, they all tend to fit well within the common designation as "conservative Protestant" (Blanchard et al. 2008; Emerson and Smith 2000; Kerley et al. 2009; Kerley, Matthews, and Shoemaker 2010; Smith 2002). The overwhelming majority attended a local congregation with relatives early in life and reported a religious conversion between ages 5 and 15. Most had been members of local religious congregations for their entire adult lives. In addition to their involvement in faith-based prison programs, the workers held leadership positions in their local congregations. Examples of these positions included pastor, minister, missionary, deacon, usher, teacher, and business manager.

After scanning Table 3.1, it would be easy to conclude that this sample of prison ministry workers is a homogenous group of conservative Protestants. As such, the inference is that the attitudes toward crime, offenders, and prison might be similar to that of most other conservative Protestants in the United States. Fortunately, there is a developing research literature on these religious adherents. The research has shown that conservative Protestants (also referred to in the literature as evangelical Christians or as fundamentalists) are more likely to support punitive crime control measures such as stricter sentences, three-strikes laws, and capital punishment. Using survey data from Oklahoma, Curry (1996) examined the relationship between conservative Protestant beliefs and perceived wrongfulness of crimes. He concluded that conservative Protestantism was positively associated with higher ratings of perceived wrongfulness of crimes when compared with other religious traditions and nonreligious orientations. Thus, both in terms of attitudes toward criminal sanctions and the seriousness of crime, evangelical Protestants often hold more punitive attitudes compared to their nonreligious and main-line counterparts.

The important question then is why conservative Protestants are more likely to be tough on crime than other religious adherents. According to Bartkowski (2001, 2004), conservative Protestants typically privilege the logic of justice over the logic of mercy. The logic of justice is focused on morality and emphasizes the punitive consequences for antisocial and criminal behaviors. By contrast, the logic of mercy stresses the importance of forgiveness of wrongdoers and highlights the many opportunities for redemption. In the context of Christianity and its Scriptures, the logic of justice distinguishes the saved from the damned. The logic of mercy, by contrast, stresses the equality of God's children, all of whom are in need of redemption. Conservative Protestants are more inclined to embrace an individualistic view of the world and to downplay the role of structural explanations for behaviors. They also focus on the consequences of sinful actions.

The conservative Protestant tendency to prioritize justice over mercy does not mean, however, that people of faith are incapable of compassion. In fact, there is growing evidence that while the logic of justice predominates in conservative Protestant congregations, it often coexists with the logic of mercy. Recent survey research reveals that religious adherents who embrace images of God as loving and forgiving are less likely to support punitive reactions to criminal offending. Using survey data from Ohio, Applegate et al. (2000) found that a literal interpretation of the Bible and a punitive image of God were significantly related to favoring punishment and opposing rehabilitation programs for offenders. Conversely, the authors found that people with stronger values of religious forgiveness were less likely to support capital punishment, and stronger attachments to religious values of forgiveness were positively associated with favoring rehabilitation and treatment.

Others have found similar results when examining religion and attitudes toward crime and offenders. Unnever, Cullen, and Applegate (2005) focus on what they call the "neglected variables" (i.e., compassion, forgiveness, and a gracious God image) from many prior studies. Using data from the 1998 General Social Survey, they found that all three measures of religious orientation were associated with being less punitive. The authors reported that those individuals who can "turn the other cheek" and are compassionate toward others are less supportive of get tough on crime policies. In a follow-up study, Unnever and Cullen (2006) investigated whether Christian fundamentalists were more likely to support capital punishment than nonfundamentalists. Their results indicated that fundamentalists hold more religiously conservative beliefs, but are more likely to express forgiveness and compassion for offenders, and are less likely to support the death penalty than nonfundamentalists.

Using data from the 2004 General Social Survey, Unnever, Cullen, and Bartkowski (2006) found that individuals who claimed to have a close relationship with a loving God were significantly less likely to support capital punishment. They surmised that the death penalty contradicts the power and purpose of God, denies offenders the opportunity for redemption, and is in opposition to the sentiment that only God can give and take away life.

## Prison Ministry Workers: What Are Their Motivations?

For most professional or volunteer activities, and especially for those that might be demanding, people are often asked the colloquial question: "Why do you do what you do?" In the case of individuals who work in a prison or volunteer in one routinely, the question is even more germane. Indeed, prison ministry workers find themselves in a unique and challenging context in which to share their faith. National-level surveys of religious congregations, such as Glenmary Research Center's Churches and Church Membership Study (2000) and Megachurches Today (Thumma, Travis, and Bird 2007), reveal that an overwhelming majority of evangelical Protestant congregations operate prison ministry outreach programs.

What these numbers do not reveal, however, is the level of participation among church members in these faith-based prison programs. Exact figures on individual-level involvement are not available, but can be estimated here. According to the national Baylor Religion Survey (Baylor University 2005), only about 20 percent of religious congregants reported "sharing their faith with strangers." Thus, if only 20 percent of local congregants typically are willing to share their faith with strangers in the general public, then presumably it is a much smaller group—likely less than 5 percent—who participate in faith-based prison programs.

When I asked one longtime local congregant about the extent of his prison ministry work, his response was intriguing:

> Well, in 1986 in the latter part of the year, my wife wanted to do something a little more and she heard about a group going to Parchman to minister to the women who were there at that time. She

went to two or three seminars and then when she came back she wanted to get more involved. So in February 1987, she and I went to an orientation at Parchman. Ever since then we, now more so me, have been involved in prison ministry. There was a time when we were going two times a month when we would go into the units to minister. My wife and another group would mostly go on Tuesday to counsel and have one-on-one relationships with some of the men in unit XX. Now, our group goes on the third Saturday of every month and we go into four units when we go. We have about 1½ hours in each unit. We split and one group goes to one unit of the morning and then another goes to another unit. In the afternoon we split up again and go into two units. So we are able to go into four units on the day that we go. So we feel like we have a good full day, especially when you drive three hours to get there and three hours to get home.

## *Compassion*

The overarching theme identified in the narratives of prison ministry workers was the compassion expressed for inmates and for their situations, especially in light of the physical, psychological, and financial costs of their ministry work. Motivations for prison ministry work fit well within the conceptual framework of moral logics (Bartkowski 2001, 2004; Hempel and Bartkowski 2008; Kerley et al. 2010). Although there is a tendency among conservative Protestants to form punitive orientations regarding punishment and public policy, the prison ministry workers I interviewed saw inmates as people just like themselves. They did not view the inmates as social outcasts. One local congregant described how he approached inmates:

> Inmates are people, so we do not look down on them. This [prison] is not a zoo. We felt there is a tendency [for volunteers] to be like tourists. We did not want people to walk in and start lecturing right away, like, "Let me tell you that you are an ignorant person, so let me tell you what you need to know."

One prison chaplain shared a similar approach to working with the inmates, which revealed a strong sense of compassion for his work:

> I wanted to work with them towards showing these men that you could change your life even though you are behind bars and that people did care about them. They were not just as the old saying [goes] "throwaways." They were still human beings that had erred, which we all have erred one way or another in life . . . and I count it a great joy to serve those men.

The interviews with prison ministry workers revealed that their attitudes toward crime control and punishment were generally in concert with those of most conservative Protestants, except that their punitive attitudes were accompanied by elements of compassion and mercy (Unnever et al. 2005, 2006). In particular, this compassion was displayed in their sensitivity to the institutional circumstances of the inmates. Although there were not justifications given for the inmates' actions that led to incarceration, there was a sensitivity of the ministry workers to the harshness of prison life and to what Sykes (1958) famously called the "pains of imprisonment." In particular, the interviewees found it important to humanize the inmates during each visit. One local congregant shared these insights:

> So often we have an attitude that people in prison are there because they deserve to be, which is a very harsh mindset. While I do not debate the fact that people have to be punished for the mistakes they make, I think it gave me a greater sensitivity that they are still people. When you actually get to sit down and talk to people and put a name with a face and realize that this person has a family, a baby, and wife, you actually start to see them as people and not just a prisoner or a number. That would probably be the bigger change that I had. It was a greater sensitivity to people and their needs. Those people are just kind of forgotten.

Over two-thirds of the ministry workers reported that they could relate not only to the harshness of prison life, but to the structural factors that led to crime. One longtime prison chaplain explained:

> The majority of folks who are in prison were in circumstances beyond their control and they just did something because when you get caught up in places, you do not know how you are going to react. If you were living on the street or if you were living in community houses, how would you react to certain things? . . . So, talking to them really made me realize that again, it really put that emphasis on it. Because they had all been in circumstances where they did something wrong and they were punished, and that is the way it is supposed to be. But, they still can be forgiven and go to Heaven.

This nuanced view of offenders typically was the result of prolonged contact with them, rather than a prior mindset. There was significant variation in the degree of compassion for inmates that the interviewees had before becoming chaplains or volunteers. Some contended that they had "had a heart" for prison ministry for as long as they could remember. The majority of interviewees, though, claimed to hold a get tough on crime mindset before their prison ministry work, but found their views refined due to extended contact with inmates. One congregant explained this change in his philosophy about prisoners:

> Sometimes when you think about people in prison, you think they killed, they robbed, they have taken advantage of somebody. But sitting there and talking to them changed the way I thought about them. It really put an emphasis on the fact that they are just like you and I. They need forgiveness just as much as you and I do. But they were in circumstances beyond their control. I believe repeat offenders become repeat offenders because we send them back into what they just left. The reason why they did those things was because they were in situations that they did not know how to handle. I really could see in a lot of those guys' eyes that they really wanted to change. They did not want to be there. They did not want to be in prison. And hopefully, some of them have enough faith in God and will have enough faith in God, that when they do get out, God will take care of them.

This shift in perceptions of offenders indicates that greater involvement in the lives of inmates and a more personal understanding of their circumstances leads those with conservative theological beliefs to draw on the underutilized values of compassion and mercy. One local congregant explained:

> People ask me why I go into the prison. Some people will say, "They [the inmates] did what they did and now they have to pay for what they did. Let them go there and rot." Well, I wish that there could really be rehabilitation. Really, there is not going to be rehabilitation until there is a saving faith. There has got to be something available because the prisons right now are nothing more than warehouses for people.

Throughout the narratives articulated by the prison ministry workers, the moral logic of compassion led them to reaffirm the humanity and worth of the inmates, established their need for redemption and a second chance, and highlighted the difficult structural circumstances they faced before going to prison. From this overarching theme of compassion for inmates and for their circumstances, three important subthemes emerged. These included: (1) prison ministry as a divine calling, (2) special connections to prison, and (3) comfort and security with inmates.

### Prison Ministry as a Divine Calling

There was unanimity among local congregants and chaplains that working in prisons was more than a public service or career path, and instead was a "divine calling" to ministry. Over half of the interviewees explained how people of faith have various spiritual gifts and that the call to prison ministry work allowed them to utilize those gifts. Interestingly, this divine calling was perceived as so powerful that they claimed it was a choice over which they had little control. One female chaplain reported that prison ministry work was an "inevitable choice." When asked why he chose prison ministry work, one local congregant replied: "I did not choose it, sir. I have no choice." He believed that prison ministry work was a divine calling for which God had specifically equipped him, and that "not just anyone could simply choose to perform it." One female congregant elaborated:

> I did not choose the ministry personally as a career just because it was what I was most familiar with. It was really something that the Lord Himself led me into, and particularly prison ministry.

Another local congregant claimed that he was called to prison ministry work, but resisted the call for many years. His main concern was for his safety while at the facilities, fueled in large part by television shows and movies that depicted prison violence. Here he described his experience:

> It is just a main calling to let those guys know that God loves them. I share this story with them that even six or seven years ago, prison scared me to death. God called me to go into prison a long time ago, but I would not go because I was scared of the stuff that goes on there. It scared me to death. Now, I want to be there, but not permanently.

A local congregant who was a stay-at-home mom said that she prayed for several weeks for God to show her "people who have a spiritual need." Subsequently she felt called to get involved with Prison Fellowship Ministries' Operation Starting Line program. She explained:

> I do not have the opportunity to be out in the world and deal with people who do not have a relationship with God. I immediately knew that working with Operation Starting Line was something I was called to do. My motive was to be around people who do not have hope in their lives.

Perhaps due to the perceived calling of these individuals to prison ministry work, their attitudes about inmates and crime control were altered over time, and they reported that compassion became the dominant force in structuring their interactions with inmates. One local congregant expressed her opinion about inmates:

> When people ask me why I go to the prison, I say that people are called to various ministries. People will say, "Look, they did what they did, and they have to pay for what they did, so let them go there and rot." But I wish that there could be rehabilitation and redemption.

### Special Connections to Prison

In addition to the divine calling to prison ministry work, the narratives revealed many special connections to prisoners or to the prison context held by local congregants and chaplains. These special connections covered a broad range of situations from working in a prison, to having a friend or relative in prison, to serving time in prison themselves. Twenty-two of the 30 prison ministry workers had these special connections. One prison chaplain explained his special connections to inmates by referring to a scriptural passage from the Gospel of Matthew:

> Like the Scripture says in Matthew's gospel where Jesus said, "I was in prison and you came to me," among those other areas of need that he talked about. I have really sensed an obligation to go and visit and try to encourage men who are locked up for any reason. It is easy to become insulated in your mind from the realities of people who are in trouble. And, for me being around men and women who are in that situation, I think serves to keep me aware of the fact in some ways, what goes on inside the walls of a church is just a very limited part of the life of a church. Worship is very important, but our mission is to touch the lives of the people who are hurting.

Many interviewees described their relationships with inmates as symbiotic. They believed that the encouragement they provided to inmates also encouraged them in their spiritual growth and fostered more positive views regarding the incarcerated. An example of the mutually beneficial nature of prison ministry work is illustrated in this local congregant's statement:

> It gives me a sense of feeling that I have helped the inmates in a small way. It has opened me up to people I did not know before. It gives me a sense of satisfaction in that I have helped to do something important to me as far as I viewed the tenants of faith. I do not think it gives me

another star in my crown, I just know that most of the guys and females in prison are hurting and are having a difficult time. I like reaching out to them with my faith.

Another local congregant, a church deacon, explained how he related prison ministry to biblical Scriptures in approaching the inmates:

I incorporated time into my daily prayer time to pray specifically for the opportunity to lead someone to Christ inside the facility. This was between 15 to 30 minutes each day. I really just did a lot of Bible study, like reading of Paul and his writings inside the prison and how he felt inside the prisons.

Seven of the interviewees described how a special connection to inmates developed from either a personal experience of incarceration or through an incarcerated relative or friend. One local congregant had a child in prison and stated that he "wanted to be real supportive of anything that will support some type of positive environment. Anything that gives the guys some sort of positive message, something they can listen to." Another local congregant recounted how he spent a brief period in prison following a "bad business deal," and then—not unlike Charles Colson—became involved with prison ministry after his release.

Another example of a special connection to prison was noted in the narratives of two local congregants, both of whom had a sibling serving time for a drug offense:

There is no way you can get through the incarceration period, especially the solitude time periods, without faith. Without knowing that God still loved him and had a plan for him that was better than prison, he could not have made it through that time period.

The second congregant explained how his philosophy about prison changed after he became involved with a prison ministry program:

It made me more cognizant to what others face in their lives and the challenges they face. It did not make me a bleeding-heart liberal, but it did make me understand that there are things that we need to do as a society. Instead of focusing on the punishment of the crime, we need to focus on the prevention of the crime. It has made me more of an activist from the standpoint of, let's focus on what we can do as Christians to prevent or to make available the sharing of faith with those who are suffering in our communities and to prevent them from ending up in the facility.

Although the conservative political orientation of the ministry workers may be linked to support for harsher punishments (Applegate et al. 2000; Britt 1998; Curry 1996; Unnever and Cullen 2006), their faith appeared to create compassion for inmates and was associated with a belief in the potential for redemption. This quote also displays a complex balancing act that evangelicals often face. Clearly, on some social issues conservative Protestants will choose to prioritize mercy and compassion over moral accountability and punitiveness.

Other interviewees became involved in prison ministry work through special connections and social networks. Several of the chaplains, for example, worked as a correctional officer prior to being hired as a chaplain or volunteering for prison ministry programs. They believed that their previous interactions with inmates, especially during times of personal or family crisis, created a unique understanding of the prison context that benefitted their ministry work. A local pastor reported that he became involved in prison ministry work after visiting an incarcerated offender who was the child of a church member.

The interviewees contended that their special connections not only made them more empathetic toward inmates, but also helped the inmates relate to them. They noted that former inmates and those with special connections to prison had "instant credibility" with inmates when they shared faith. The mantra that "people don't care how much you know until they know how much you care" was popular among the interviewees. One prison chaplain explained:

> I think that one of the key elements is the fact that many of the participants have, through their own life experience, been able to relate to the plight of the offenders both before and during their incarceration. I like the fact that they bring in those who were incarcerated themselves or whose lives have been impacted because someone near and dear to them has been incarcerated. So there is a level of relativity that may not be there with someone like myself. It has really surprised me how quickly I have been received, but I still think that it is such a wonderful thing, and an altogether different thing when someone has come here and they said, "Hey brother, I was incarcerated in this facility or that facility and this was my experience, and this is what Jesus has done for me." When a person talks experientially, there is just a difference there.

## Comfort and Security with Inmates

A final aspect of compassion observed in the narratives is the interviewees' sense of comfort and security in the prison context. Many investigators and former inmates have described the deleterious features of prison life (Hassine 1999; Irwin 1985), and religious and nonreligious individuals alike often are reticent even to visit a prison. Nevertheless, nearly all prison ministry workers interviewed here reported an inherent sense of comfort spending time in prisons regardless of the demographic characteristics or criminal histories of the inmates. They did not appear to share the view of prisoners as predators or animals as promulgated in some media depictions and conservative political discourse. Perhaps because they believed that prison ministry was a divine calling, they felt at ease even in the most dangerous of prisons. They reported an attempt to be on the same level as the inmates and their genuine concern for inmates allayed fears they had about working in prisons. One chaplain explained how he dealt with being in the prison context:

> Basically, I have done pretty decent with them because I come down to a level of talking with them that they can comprehend. So, I relate pretty well with my inmates, and probably one of the reasons is they know that I care. I am going to do my best to help them. There are other chaplains that are sort of standoffish, but I will walk into wherever. I don't care how many guys are in the zone [term used for each building that houses inmates]. When I go into the zone, the door closes behind me, and I am in there with 120 or whatever guys, and that is okay because that is what it is all about.

A local congregant recalled her thoughts after the first visit to prison:

> I was really surprised about how things were. It just seemed like a regular place where we could talk to people about Christ. The only difference [between us and them] is that we could leave after it was over. We really felt comfortable around the guys. It was not scary like you often hear about prisons.

This sense of comfort with being in the prison context was displayed in how easily the interviewees interacted with inmates. Rather than interacting in a tentative or standoffish manner, they tried to be engaging with the inmates. They also found it important to interact on equal footing, and without projecting themselves as authoritative or superior. One local congregant explained:

> At one facility we did the one-on-one. I actually went to the cells. I treated their cells like their homes. I did not enter unless they asked or sit on their bed unless they said I could. When I am talking to them, it is like talking to my neighbor, no different.

Another local congregant had a very similar approach:

I do not see an offender, I see a soul. I see a soul and whatever they are dealing with[,] . . . they decided, "I am going to try this Jesus thing. I am making the decision for Christ." So, I want to do all that is within my God-given ability to reach that person so they can become an effective disciple of Jesus Christ.

## Prison Ministry Workers: What Are Their Goals and Expectations?

### Goal Orientation

To this point I have explored the backgrounds of prison ministry workers and their motivations for ministry work. In this final section, I explore the goals and expectations for their work. In considering how evangelical Christians might approach prison ministry work, I anticipated that they would have specific, and perhaps lofty, numeric goals for religious conversions of inmates. This expectation is based on scriptural accounts of mass conversions (e.g., the report by the Apostle Peter of about 3,000 conversions during Pentecost), as well as modern examples such as the Billy Graham Crusades. Likewise, I anticipated that accounts of large-scale conversions would structure the goals of prison ministry workers and lead to disappointment if their work did not produce such results (Kerley, Matthews, and Shoemaker 2009).

Contrary to these expectations, however, the chaplains and local congregants interviewed here reported tempered goals for their ministry work. They appeared to be satisfied with just the opportunity to interact with inmates and rarely developed numeric goals. One local congregant, who had worked with prison ministry programs for over thirty years, summarized his goals for each prison visit this way:

No sir, we don't establish any numbers and we don't go and pray for any numbers or anything like that because this is not our show. We go in and we are all teammates. We are not counselors or super-educated people. All we know is that Jesus loves us and has a plan for our lives. He tells us the rules that we must follow so that is what we ask for since this is God's show that He controls and puts people in our face to speak to. We call it a divine appointment and that is what we look for, and we don't pressure anybody into making a decision. We are not there to get names on a piece of paper.

The ministry workers presented a nuanced view of the goals and expectations for their work. On the one hand, they wanted to witness a large number of prisoners committing to faith as a result of their activities. On the other hand, they felt a need to temper their expectations. One chaplain described the balance between hoping for large-scale conversions and being realistic about numeric goals:

> How can I put a number on who is saved? I would love to see everybody saved. My goal was that God told me to be there and I was gonna help to spread the word that He wants us to spread. So, no, I don't guess I had a number that I wanted to see saved. If one is saved, that's plenty for me. Because it's worth it.

Of the 30 ministry workers interviewed, only one mentioned having numeric goals before entering the prison, but then toned down her expectations upon arrival. She summarized her approach and changing goals:

> In the back of my mind I just wanted to see hundreds and hundreds of people accept Christ through the opportunity to go inside the prisons. That was an initial thought as I got involved. When I visited the first facility I realized that it was just comforting to comfort the people who were kind of beaten down inside the prison, and it was to bring new people to accept Jesus. When I first got involved I had an unrealistic thought as to what I wanted it to be. From the first few hours I was in the facility, I realized this [comforting] is what I needed to be doing.

Even with lofty numeric goals in mind at the beginning of her ministry work, this local congregant suggested that her goals quickly moved away from numbers and toward building relationships. For all of the interviewees, the avoidance of numeric goals was tied to the belief that they were "serving God" through their work in prison regardless of the number of religious conversions.

## Being Used by God

The important question to address now is *why* the chaplains and local congregants would go to great lengths to avoid thought or discussion of numeric goals in their ministry work. The interviewees appeared to craft a narrative in which their evangelistic efforts were part of a larger process, and not a stand-alone effort. The ministry workers claimed that they did not feel pressure to create or achieve certain numeric goals for conversions because they viewed themselves as part of a process in which all persons of faith—what they commonly called the "body of Christ"—have responsibility to share faith with others.

Using this rationale, no single person of faith is expected to lead large numbers to a religious conversion, but all are expected to be part of the process. Their primary goal was simply to be "used by God" by going into prisons to share faith and to encourage inmates. One local congregant described her approach to every prison visit:

> I guess I had some goals going in. Mainly just to be faithful. To go in there and let God direct me as He wants to. I wanted to be able to share the gospel with people and to encourage people who were already Christians. I wanted God to give me the strength to talk to people about him.

A local pastor summarized his approach as follows:

> We just tried to get everyone focused to share the gospel with as many people as we could and we let God work out the numbers. If we are faithful to Him and follow Him, He will lead people to Him.

Another church leader mirrored this approach:

> Whenever I go into a prison, I always ask God to humble me and He always does a good job of that. I want Him to be sure my motives are right. I don't want it to be something that I am doing. I want God's spirit through me to work and I want to be used by God.

One local congregant, who just recently became involved in prison ministry work, claimed that God seemed to take control of her thoughts and words each time she visited a facility:

> Well, it's quite extraordinary when you've been through the experience and you realize that the Lord put things in your heart and in your mind to say. It's almost as if it wasn't you, but the Lord working through you. When one realizes that this has happened and you have been an instrument of God, in my opinion, that is pretty close to the ultimate experience from a human standpoint, to be used by the very one that created you.

In nearly every narrative, the ministry workers described this process with horticultural analogies. Frequently they used concepts such as "planting seeds," "watering plants," "producing fruit," and "harvesting." They saw themselves as a small part of a larger process and thus were able to temper their goals and expectations for prison conversions. One veteran chaplain used this analogy:

> We don't expect to reach everybody in our unit. We have help in the body of Christ to help with the same goal. I may just be watering now. I may have just planted a seed, and here comes somebody with a prison fellowship program and they may be watering. Then another group comes in and brings in the harvest. But all of us poured into this individual.

By viewing themselves as part of a preordained and mutually reinforcing process, the ministry workers I interviewed could cope with the disappointment of limited responses during their visits. One longtime chaplain, who was in a management position at his facility, summarized:

> I have found in the past that it tends to go better if I don't worry about the details. The Lord will take care of that and I just respond as I feel the Holy Spirit is leading in a particular situation. If it turns out to be quite a few that is great, but if it turns out to be one or two that's fine. I even try not to be discouraged if I don't see any fruits from the conversation, because there are things that the inmates can take back and think about.

A local congregant echoed this sentiment:

> We just really don't set numeric goals and I don't think that they would be wise to set. While we would like to have more people to come to the meetings than we have, we have found out if we were dependent upon numbers we would have probably dropped the ministry a long time ago.

### Sharing and Encouragement

Related to this theme of being used by God is the focus on encouragement in the narratives of the ministry workers. When religious adherents discuss issues of faith with others, typically it is referred to in evangelical Christian discourse as "sharing your faith" or simply as "sharing" (Ingram 1989; Tuttle 1999). In many cases, sharing may be expressly evangelical when a religious adherent encourages a nonreligious individual to attend a religious service or consider conversion. In other cases, however, sharing may involve a religious person helping someone deal with problems regardless of the person's spiritual state.

Sharing faith often is difficult for local religious congregants because it challenges the belief systems of others and places them in a powerless position of needing to be saved by someone else (Ingram 1989). The ministry workers I interviewed routinely avoided the labels of "soul savers" or "soul winners" and instead saw their main purpose as providing encouragement to inmates. One local congregant summarized his approach as follows:

I guess because of my experiences, I just see it as an opportunity to go in and talk to the guys one-on-one. I guess from my journey in life, I feel a connection with the guys. So, I just see it as an opportunity to go in and share my perspective because I want to share with them on any kind of level. I guess anytime somebody mentions goals I think of numbers. Now at the end, I guess everybody likes to tally up numbers, but I don't ever and the people that I am involved with don't look at numbers. I guess we wish we could talk to everybody.

Another local congregant had a similar method:

I want to be real supportive of anything that will support some type of positive environment. Anything that gives the guys some sort of positive message, something they can listen to, and say, "Gosh, it's not all junk and depravity," like they experience in the prison every night.

Religious congregants, in particular those categorized as conservative Protestants, often are thought to be pious and high-minded in their interactions with unbelievers. There is even an approach common among these religious adherents known as "confrontational evangelism." In stark contrast, however, the ministry workers I interviewed were careful to frame their interactions with inmates in a basic and nonthreatening manner. Routinely the workers described their strategy for prison ministry as "a simple plan" (Kerley, Matthews, and Shoemaker 2009). Consider this example:

And don't think that you've got to get fancy with the Word with them. These guys don't need fanciness, they need truth, and sometimes you have some of these that come in and man, you know, they are flamboyant and everything like that, but they don't necessarily have sight of what the guys really need. And sometimes that can be a factor that the guys don't get what they need because these people think that they should be a higher level or something like that, and it just has to be a down-to-earth thing with these guys.

In fact, one chaplain expressed reservations about some ministry groups, in particular national ones, who visited his prison:

> Some national ministry groups are pretty superficial. They barely serve a purpose because they treat the inmate the way he's used to hearing people: preach at him, at him, at him, at him. I don't think they get it. They're not nearly as concerned about this person's whole life as they are about getting a number of people to walk the aisle. And that's not a judgment, that's just what I see.

## Avoidance of Denominational Issues

The second major theme to emerge from the narratives is that chaplains and local congregants stressed the need to avoid denominational issues when interacting with inmates. Although evangelical Protestant congregations, particularly in the South, are often painted with a broad brush as homogeneous, there are many factors that make them distinctive (Bartkowski 2001; Smith 2002; Woodberry and Smith 1998). Issues such as versions and interpretations of Scriptures, baptism, communion, style of dress, women in the ministry, and roles of husbands and wives in marriage often are debated in conservative Protestant congregations.

In the prison context, the chaplains and local congregants I interviewed described how they crafted a simple message of hope and encouragement to share faith with inmates. The ministry workers were cognizant of the fact that their message of faith must be simple and free of the "shackles of denominationalism," as one interviewee described it. One local minister described his approach:

> We don't go in there and try to get them to join the Baptist or Methodist church or what have you. We just go in and share about Jesus and how that relationship needs to develop. We stay away from religious things and requirements that [a] church will place upon a person. We just want them to know that the basic things that they need to know is that Jesus loves them, has a plan for their life, and there is only one to follow and that is Jesus Christ.

A prison chaplain echoed this approach:

> We do not emphasize personal theology. We represent the Christian, if we are Christian chaplains, and we represent the Christian theology and not our denominational theology. Now if someone asks me about my denomination, I am happy to discuss it with them, but we do not discuss or promote our own personal beliefs.

The ministry workers attempt to create a message that revolves around faith in God, but does not take into account denominational distinctions. Their rationale is that inmates' religious backgrounds should be respected, and to get involved in discussions of denominational issues would be to obfuscate the simple message of faith and hope. One chaplain explained her nondenominational approach to prison ministry work:

> One thing about Protestant Christianity as well as Catholicism is that we all agree that Jesus is Lord, we all agree that we are to take an example [from] the life of Christ, and do what we can to access the enabling presence of God and manifest the fruit of the Spirit. If we just do that, that takes up all our time, so we really don't have to have time to debate on the more trivial topics.

It was routine for the ministry workers to discuss the importance of being respectful and open to all religious beliefs that the inmates held. One local congregant summarized this approach:

> We've agreed that Jesus is Lord, let's focus on that. You know, so I try to concentrate on the key fundamentals of the faith, and everything else, I try to let the guys be open, even if you don't believe the same thing, at least understand why he believes as he believes. It's good to be open-minded. I don't have to agree, but we can agree to disagree in peace.

A chaplain made a similar point:

> You've got to be open. Different people have different beliefs and so you need to respect them and then find out where they're at, try to help them [any] way you can. I'm not trying to make a Baptist out of anybody.

## Meeting People "Where They Are"

The next question from this theme is *why* ministry workers are reticent to broach denominational issues. Two explanations emerged from the narratives. First, the ministry workers perceived that their calling to prison ministry required that they interact with inmates in a simple and caring manner, and one free from religious pretense and judgment. Rather than expecting inmates to conform to a specific set of denominational tenets, the ministry workers focused instead on the similarities among myriad beliefs. The workers spoke of interacting with inmates "where they are" and "on their level" rather than coming from a place of piety. One chaplain described his ministry work this way: "I just see it as an opportunity to go in and meet them where they are and share my perspective because I want to share with them on any kind of level." Another chaplain described it this way:

> We are very insistent that we are all in one accord and we all accept that. We are doing the same thing with one thing in mind, we are saying things that are from Scriptures that they need to hear and understand. I am saying we do the basic things and stay away from the theological or postgraduate works. We want to meet them where they are and guide them step-by-step to a higher level by the time we leave them on the weekend.

Perhaps most important for the ministry workers was the recognition of their own varying religious backgrounds compared to those of the inmates they served. From that standpoint, different religious backgrounds demanded respect and not justification. One local congregant described his approach to competing doctrines:

> Well, there's so many viewpoints for one thing and a lot of the guys that are here, many of them have burned out on church. . . . And they're wanting to get away from it and so what you've got to do is get them away from that rebellion and say . . . we don't have an established church though we are going to have a church building. But we don't have a denominational church here, it's going to be open for everyone. So what we have to do is find a happy medium in there for them that will meet their need and teach them and train them and everything.

This local congregant reasoned that many inmates had become disenchanted and turned off by the piety and denominationalism of many local congregations, and thus she wanted to present a simple message of faith. The chaplains in the study dealt with this issue on a daily basis. They asserted that they must respect the belief systems of inmates and find a way to encourage them from that point. One chaplain argued:

> You have to be mostly transparent. You can't be old hard-lined Baptist or hard-lined whatever. You have to realize they have different beliefs than we do and that's why our boss's attitude is "perform or provide." If we can't perform a service for them, we've got to provide somebody who can.

One new chaplain elaborated and discussed the concept of religious tolerance:

> I have no problem with all different faiths speaking to the inmates once the religious group has been told that everyone has an opinion and you don't have to shout to make yours better than his. . . . We help out the people who want help, whether it be spiritual or otherwise, and we work as team. It's just called tolerance. I give you yours and you give me mine and we're going to be friends.

Although it would be easy to gravitate toward only inmates from similar backgrounds, one veteran chaplain made it clear that his duty was to serve all inmates, and not just those who identified with a particular religious tradition:

> The chaplain role here is for all people. . . . I minister to people of all faith. My religious belief is to help them get assistance here to help them with their religious preference. Whoever wants sacrament, whoever wants to be baptized, whoever needs religious counseling, that's my job regardless of what faith he is.

## Conflict Prevention

Another reason why chaplains and local congregants were careful to avoid denominational issues was to prevent verbal or physical conflicts. It should come as no surprise that the discussion of specific denominational issues—whether in the general public or in prison—can cause serious problems. The ministry workers suggested that a focus on denominational issues could create two types of conflict in prisons.

First, inmates might become confused or upset by such discussions and avoid faith-based programs. One local congregant active in Bill Glass Ministries prison programs said this:

> We don't get into doctrine or denominational issues. We prefer that to never come up. They're usually things that bring about strife and disagreement. I know that I see it that way, and I think I can say that Bill Glass tries to steer everyone away from that. Bill Glass Ministries is not about doctrines and it's not about theologies outside the core beliefs that most of us see as the Christian faith.

Another local congregant made a similar statement:

> We took a tactful approach and made the conversation low key, looked for openings to start witnessing, started a spiritual discussion, but

didn't force the issue, but be tactful about it. Just like you would with anybody else. You would be sensitive to where the situation was and where the conversation was headed. Be as sensitive in that kind of environment as you would with anybody else.

Although the prison ministry workers in this study reported that they avoided denominational issues, they had many experiences with other chaplains and local congregants who did not share their approach. One longtime prison volunteer recalled major problems from a recent trip:

There were some church folks who got side-tracked talking about denominational distinctions and [were] going out on a tangent. We don't like the negative impact that has on inmates . . . because our intent is to encourage volunteers to stay on track and not go off on denominational or doctrinal differences.

Similarly, a local pastor recalled:

Sometimes a volunteer will say there's only one way to Heaven and nobody can be saved otherwise. Then that brings division. It usually makes inmates offended and that causes them to lose interest in faith.

These negative experiences reinforced their belief in the importance of avoiding denominational issues. The ministry workers believed in keeping their message and interactions positive, and were fearful that they might be perceived as stumbling blocks if they decided to delve into denominational issues.

Second, the discussion of divisive denominational issues could create conflict in the form of arguments and fights between inmates or between, between inmates and ministry workers, and between inmates and correctional staff. One veteran chaplain offered this observation:

I don't know if it's just tradition or it's in the policy that we are not allowed to bring up something that would create a problem for security in the zone in which you get inmates really physically arguing. We don't allow them to get vocal about that, we just accept what they say and make it not a point of argument at all.

Another chaplain asserted:

We have to be nondenominational in what we say and there's times that your belief could get in the way if you allowed it to because you don't always agree with what somebody else might say, but you never condemn what they say. You tell the individual, you listen to them and accept what you think is right. I mean, that's the way it has to be and you don't want any physical problems to come up.

## Summary

Although conservative Protestant congregations, especially in the South, long have been associated with volunteer work in their local communities, faith-based prison programs appear to be under the purview of a tiny subset of religious congregants. Recall that national-level surveys indicate widespread existence of such programs, but low rates of participation. Based on all available data, my estimate is that, on average, no more than 5 percent of local church members are involved actively in a prison ministry program. In this chapter I examined prison ministry workers who organize and deliver faith-based prison programs in Mississippi. My analysis was based on 30 in-depth interviews with prison chaplains and local religious congregants. I addressed three important questions: (1) Who are these people? (2) What are their motivations? (3) What are their goals and expectations?

At first glance my interviewees appeared to be typical conservative Protestant congregants based on their demographic and religious backgrounds. Yet throughout the narratives I observed that the moral logic of compassion emerged as the overarching theme for understanding their motivations to work in prisons. From this overarching theme of compassion for inmates and for their circumstances, three important subthemes emerged: (1) the calling of prison ministry, (2) special connections to prison, and (3) comfort and security with inmates. These results were somewhat unexpected, and I think make a considerable contribution to the literature. Many studies over the past decade have called into question some of the prevailing wisdom (most of it pejorative) about conservative Protestants, and my results are in line with those studies.

Many will recall the 2000 presidential campaign when candidate George Walker Bush presented himself as a "compassionate conservative." The idea, at least as I recall it, was that he could support conservative fiscal and social policies, but do so without the perceived callousness or elitism of others in his party. While it is not clear whether the eventual two-term president's mantra had any real meaning, the concept is a fascinating one. My contention is that if compassionate conservatives exist, the prison ministry workers I interviewed must be exemplars. The ability to look beyond a criminal to see a spiritual soul is an exceptional quality these interviewees possessed, and perhaps it is what allowed them to be so comfortable in the prison context.

It seems clear from my analysis that the religious convictions and practices of conservative Protestants are complex, and not simple reflections of a punitive world view. Local congregants who focus on individualism and moral accountability prioritize the logic of justice in forming their crime control attitudes. Congregants who focus on compassion and redemption prioritize the logic of mercy. The prison ministry workers appear to favor mercy on this continuum of justice versus mercy (Kerley et al. 2010).

In terms of the goals and expectations of the prison ministry workers, chaplains and local congregants had a distinctive goal orientation that discouraged the creation of numeric goals. The workers were also careful to avoid denominational issues that could distract from sharing their faith and providing encouragement to inmates. Instead, they crafted what they frequently referred to as a "simple plan" for their "simple faith." To prevent inmates from losing interest in faith and to avoid potential verbal or physical conflicts, chaplains and local congregants in the study were careful to avoid hot-button issues in their interactions with inmates (Kerley, Matthews, and Shoemaker 2009).

# 4

# The Conversion Experience

Discussions of religion in correctional contexts often include questions about the authenticity of religious conversion and commitment. Skeptics of jailhouse conversion often assert that inmates will claim a religious conversion or attend religious services only to obtain special privileges, to get out of their cells or units for an extended time, to front illegal activities, or to get credit for good behavior that will facilitate early release. Others claim that faith-based prison programs should be on par with traditional secular programs, and claim in some cases that faith is the only legitimate pathway to recovery and rehabilitation.

I will not deny that there are seemingly countless examples of disingenuous religious behavior in prison. Given the national recidivism rate of 67 percent (BJS 2002), for every one success story of a reformed prisoner there are two stories of failure. That being said, prison officials at the state and federal level have yet to develop faith detectors to verify the veracity of inmates' claims of religious conversion. Doing so clearly would be a nice complement to the metal detectors already used in most prisons. Consequently, our goal as social scientists—and my goal in this chapter—is to understand the process and perceived impact of religious conversion among inmates.

Charles Colson may be the best-known jailhouse convert. Having just passed away in April 2012, Colson has received much attention from scholars, practitioners, and media who study crime and the criminal justice system. Colson's story is fascinating in that he was a public figure with two very different phases of life. In phase one, Colson was a promising graduate of George Washington University Law School in 1959 and quickly made partner in a major law firm. He parlayed this experience into an appointment as special counsel to the president under Richard Nixon. Widely regarded as the "hatchet man" for Nixon, Colson was a key member of the Watergate Seven in the major scandal that would lead to the president's resignation in 1974. While an extremely apprehensive Colson was facing indictment in 1973 for obstruction of justice and expecting to receive a prison sentence, the story goes that a friend gave him the book *Mere Christianity* by well-known evangelical author C. S. Lewis. After reading the book, Colson claimed to experience a religious conversion. Thus, the venerable prison conversion technically did not occur in prison, but just before.

In phase two, Colson reported to a federal prison in Alabama to serve a sentence of one to three years. He would serve only seven months and allegedly was a model prisoner during his stint. While in prison Colson began writing his memoirs. in which he described his lack of ethics in business and politics juxtaposed against his newfound religious faith. The culminating book, *Born Again*, was published in 1976. In that same year Colson founded Prison Fellowship Ministries (PFM), which currently is the largest prison ministry organization in the United States. The goal of the organization is to facilitate religious programs, to coordinate outreach and aftercare efforts, and to provide Christmas gifts for the children of inmates. Colson would publish over a dozen other books, including *Life Sentence*, which was first published in 1979. He spent the remainder of his life working with PFM and creating a radio ministry to discuss various faith-based issues in society.

The story of Colson's religious conversion certainly is a dramatic one. To go from hotshot attorney to disgraced political operative, prisoner, and finally director of a major organization devoted to helping the incarcerated is remarkable. Colson's narrative of prison conversion has served as a heuristic device for the way in which many in the general public, and even those in academia, understand religious faith in correctional settings. Depending on the religious and political persuasion of readers, Colson's story may be the ideal type for supporters of faith-based prison programs or the exception that proves the rule for skeptics.

The issues of when and under what circumstances individuals experience a religious conversion have long fascinated scholars of religion, as well as clergy and laity. In *The Varieties of Religious Experience,* William James was one of the first modern scholars to explore the complexities of religious conversion. His characterization of conversion as an "explosion of subliminal tension" underscores its complexity (James 1902, p. 237). He explains further: "To say that a man is 'converted' means . . . that religious ideas, previously peripheral in his consciousness, now take a central place, and that religious aims form the habitual centre of his energy" (James 1902, p. 165). Much later, Brock (1962, p. 198) concluded that among those who have experienced it, "religious conversion is frequently so rich and unique as to defy adequate description."

Doing my best to remain undaunted by the difficult task, and armed with all of the methodological tools of the social sciences, I set out in this chapter to explore the contours of religious conversion in correctional contexts. To do so I draw on 173 in-depth interviews with prison inmates and residents of halfway houses in Alabama and Mississippi. As described in detail in the Appendix, 63 interviews were conducted with inmates in Mississippi's largest men's prison, 40 interviews were conducted with inmates in Alabama's largest women's prison, and 70 interviews were conducted with women in a halfway house in Alabama.

## The Timing of Conversion

The first important issue to address is whether religious conversion tends to occur as a single moment of spiritual awareness, or as a gradual process that leads a higher spiritual state. Scholarly research on this topic has been inconclusive, with support found for both outcomes. Within most evangelical Protestant faith traditions, however, the answer is clear. They tend to place a high priority on a single moment of religious conversion, or what they call being "born again" or "saved" (Mahoney and Pargament 2004; Zinnbauer and Pargament 1998). Clergy and laity alike often reference scriptural stories—such as the dramatic conversion of Saul (later known as Paul the Apostle) on the road to Damascus, of Peter while fishing, or of the "thief on the cross" beside Jesus—to demonstrate how conversion must occur at one moment in time. According to this view, religious conversion must take place in a single moment but religious maturation (commonly called "sanctification") is a gradual process.

Clearly there are few individuals who will have the dramatic experience of Saul, who was blinded temporarily by a supernatural light and then heard the voice of God, but it appears from my analysis of the 173 narratives that the large majority (about 80 percent) of those claiming to be religious converts described their conversion as a single moment, and not as a gradual process. One inmate from Parchman prison described the conversion that occurred near the beginning of his first prison stint:

> Well, [I was converted] when I first got locked up. I was so far down that I got on my knees and asked God to save me really without any feeling or knowing that he had raised me up. I really didn't feel it, but a drastic change took place. You know I honored His word and he

raised me up and I've been on track since '94. I was saved in '94. I was really in bad shape.

A woman inmate from Tutwiler prison described a similar experience of conversion around the same time:

> At this time, it was in '95, and I was in jail. It was the middle of the night. Everybody was asleep. I'd been going to church. You know, I read the Scripture, John 3:16 and all the Scriptures that followed it, and I just believed what His word said, you know. I fell on my knees. You know, I cried out to Him. And [from] that point on, in that jail, I just had a peace where I was at.

Another woman inmate recalled her conversion experience only a few weeks after beginning her sentence:

> And so finally one day we had a church service, and I remember I was sleeping. I didn't want to get up, I was tired. I was still in what we call my "drug coma," and I had only been there for a few weeks. And I made myself get up and go. And after the service, I remember it was the first time that I felt the spirit in a long time. And after the service, I went back to my cell, and I was alone in my cell. And I just got down on my knees at the foot of my bed and just gave it up. I just let it go. I said [to God]: "I just don't know what to do anymore. I'm tired. I just don't know what to do. But if you want me, you can have me." And so things began to change in my life. He gave me my family back.

These descriptions were typical among those who had been incarcerated for any significant length of time. Frequently they referenced a specific time when they "reached out to God," or "cried out to God" and asked for salvation. It was common for interviewees to reference the year, their age, and even the exact date when the conversion occurred. I also noted how for nearly half of the 70 women interviewed at the halfway house, they could recall the exact date of their conversion experience, and referred to it proudly as their "second birth" or "second birthday." One woman recalled her conversion experience just before being court-ordered to the halfway house:

> I didn't really realize it [immediately] but I gave my life to the Lord before that night, before I come up here. I was like, "Lord, if you could just get me to Birmingham I promise I won't leave. I'll stay." And so that's what I did. It really saved my life, you know what I mean? And since I been here I been doing a lot better. I got saved and got baptized, and then you know I'm really tryin' to change my life for the better cause the way I was living, it's just not the way to live.

Although the large majority of in-prison conversion experiences occurred during or after regular religious services or activities in the facility, there were some cases of inmates making faith commitments in response to events sponsored by national prison ministry programs. One Parchman inmate described his conversion experience immediately after hearing a speaker from Operation Starting Line (OSL), which was a program created by Prison Fellowship Ministries. This is how he described the words of the guest speaker, along with his reaction:

> He [the speaker] had said, he said, "Hold on let me speak this: 'As the birds and the flowers, as these things be such, know that you are much more valuable to me than these here things are.'" I remember[ed] that, and I said, "Well if this be the truth, you know, and He [God] just did this here, so, we've got to be a lot more valuable to the Lord. That's what I thought, you know. So, at that time, like I say, I believe that's when I really gave my life to the Lord."

Finally, some inmates claimed that their conversion experience was the culmination of one or more "false conversions" or "false starts." One inmate described how earlier in life he was baptized in his local church, but realized later that his "faith was not real." He said that he did not experience a genuine conversion until soon after going to prison:

> But since I've been here I have received the gospel of the grace of God by faith. See [back] then, I only did it [baptism] because that's what I was told to do. I didn't understand salvation . . . I was going through tradition. Tradition will condemn a man, but then when I heard the gospel of the grace of God since I've been locked up this time, I got saved. And, I received Christ's death burial, resurrection for the payment of my sins, [and I'm] never alone. And, God transformed me.

### The Emotions of Conversion

Closely related to the timing of conversion are the emotions and psychic states of individuals at conversion. It is easy to imagine a wide range of emotions that might be experienced by the average convert. Given the focus on confession of sin in evangelical Protestant doctrines, emotions such as contrition, sadness, anxiety, and guilt are common. The practice of alter calls and the creation of a section called the "mourners' bench" in local Protestant congregations highlight this point. Some researchers have argued that the conversion experience is rooted in conflict or crisis. Johnson (1959, p. 117), for example, asserts:

A genuine religious conversion is the outcome of a crisis. Though it may occur to persons in a variety of circumstances and forms, and though we may find many preparatory steps and long-range consequences, the event of conversion comes to focus in a crisis of ultimate concern. There is in such conversion a sense of desperate conflict in which one is so involved that his whole meaning and destiny are at stake in a life-or-death, all-or-none significance.

Johnson's summary is instructive in terms of framing the conversion narratives of prison inmates and residents of halfway houses. Similarly, Zinnbauer and Pargament (1998, p. 163) explain:

The religious convert [is] someone who is experiencing great difficulty in his or her life. In an attempt to deal with the situation, the convert realizes that something is wrong. The old self and way of life are seen as inadequate, and the only solution is to seek a radical change.

Perhaps the most representative description of the feeling of crisis among my interviewees came from an inmate at Parchman who was near the beginning of a lengthy sentence for a violent crime. Note in particular the sense of guilt, brokenness, and hopelessness he felt prior to his religious conversion:

I was doin' a lot of wicked things. Anyway, I fell on my knees in that cell one day and was heartbroken and cryin'. I ain't ever been this alone. I had nobody. I was one of those people that have people around. It hurt me. I cried out to God that day and it seem like God spoke to my heart, "Man get up off the floor. You do what you know to be right, now rest." That's when I got saved. The Bible said, "Whosoever call upon the Lord shall be saved." I called on Him. He saved me.

Another inmate at Parchman discussed at length how prior to his conversion he was "locked up physically and spiritually." After his conversion, however, he described an overarching sense of peace and freedom:

Trustin' what God told me, in His word. And it frees me, it makes me feel confident that God will never leave me alone. God won't lie. He said, "I cannot lie. If you would serve me then I would give you that life more abundantly," and the life it comin' with that self-confidence, of mental perspective, saying, well, "God is for me, who can be against me?" I feel free on the inside. You know, I can look at things now and I can even look at the world and say, "Wow, . . . it's a mad mayhem." You know, granted another party is going on. You know,

I'm glad that I actually got things right with God and that now I have a sense of peace and freedom.

The conversion experiences of women from the prison and halfway house had a similar flavor in terms of negative emotions and emotional states immediately preceding them. Frequently they referenced being depressed and even at a "crisis point" in describing their experience. Note in this exchange how the woman describes a decline in her physical and emotional self and how she claims that her faith commitment made a difference:

> *Participant*: Like I said, [before conversion] I had dealt with a lot of things before I came in here and I have always taken care of myself. I mean my appearance and that sort of thing. I have always been very conscientious of that sort of thing, but with depression and everything I was going through, I wasn't taking the time. I mean, of course I still bathed and did everything I needed to do hygiene wise, but um, but yeah, I did change. I have changed as far as I am taking pride in myself again.
> *Interviewer*: So do you think the emphasis on religion has been a big part of your change?
> *Participant*: Definitely, definitely. It has definitely had a very big part. I don't think I could have [changed.] I would not be the person now changed on the inside and the outside if it weren't for [my] faith and the emphasis [at the center] on Christianity.

The crisis point for many of the women was related not only to their situation in terms of crime and illegal drugs and the resulting incarceration, but also to a crisis point in their families. One Tutwiler inmate recounted the story of her conversion experience shortly after making a phone call to her hometown:

> I had called home. The cost [was] like $18–20 to call, and they told me my mom had a stroke. And when they said my mom had a stroke, I just gave everything to the Lord. I called out, I said, "Lord, I just submit everything to you. I sacrifice all the things that I like to do, and I give it to you. Smoking cigarettes, cussing, playing con games. Just doing everything." I gave everything to the Lord. And it's been five years now, just totally with the Lord. In fact, I was just a chapel worker out there, so God is good.

Overall, what the narratives here suggest is that strong emotional states appear to be in play just before and just after the moment of religious conversion. The interviewees claimed to transition quickly from extreme states of conflict, crisis, sadness, anxiety, shamefulness, or hopelessness (or all of those simultaneously) to states of freedom, joy, relief, fulfillment, or peace (or all of those simultaneously). Pargament (1997, p. 248), perhaps the best-known modern scholar on faith-based coping, explains it this way: "Existence itself has become the problem and a fundamental change is called for. The object of conversion is to transform an entire life, to create a substantive change in both destinations and pathways of living."

What is most fascinating from my perspective is that interviewees claimed that their extreme emotional shift occurred in only the time it took them to sense a need for a higher power, confess wrongdoing, and commit to a relationship with that higher power. I also observed that most of the reported conversions occurred while the interviewees were in prison or a halfway house, and they occurred in the midst of major troubles and low points in their lives, or what most called "rock bottom." My analysis of the interviews thus suggests that the majority of the conversions had all of the crisis and drama of Saul's conversion, but without the bright lights and audible voice of God.

## A New Faith-Based Identity

Religious converts, whether in prison or in free society, typically report a radical change that is characterized by major shifts in "attitudes, thoughts, and self-understandings" (Maruna, Wilson, and Curran 2006, p. 162). In their meta-review of studies of conversion, Snow and Machalek (1984, p. 169) concluded that "the notion of radical change remains at the core of all conceptions of conversion." Stanley (1965, p. 60) noted that "religious conversion has often been considered to be caused by a type of temporary neurotic condition, resolution of which results in the establishment of a 'new life.'" In the modern religious vernacular, religious conversions routinely are accompanied by a shift in how "saved" individuals interpret their past when they were "lost."

Religious converts also tend to construct a "prosocial narrative identity" that can account for why their prior actions were not true reflections of self and why their present and future actions have new meaning. Routinely converts will describe their criminal and deviant pasts as "not me" or "not the real me." Maruna, Wilson, and Curran (2006, p. 180) suggest that when offenders create a narrative identity, it may "integrate disparate and shameful life events into a coherent, empowering whole, renew prisoners' sense of their own personal biography, and provide them with hope and a vision for the future." Thus, previous research on religious inmates highlights the importance of conversion in creating a new sense of self to cope with the struggles of prison life (Maruna, Wilson, and Curran 2006; Ward and Marshall 2007). The dominant framework for making sense of their lives and for moving forward in positive directions thus may be a constant comparison of the old and new self.

I found evidence of the juxtaposition between the old and new self throughout the narratives. It was observed routinely among men and women offenders, and among those in prisons and in halfway houses. One male inmate described a clear difference between his previous life of drugs and crime and his new life of faith. In doing so, he quoted nearly verbatim a Scripture from 2 Corinthians to support his approach (although he mistakenly attributes the quote to Zechariah). The inmate explained his new identity this way:

> Now I tell people, "Don't go back there, back selling drugs, back to the old you. Be a new you now! Cause Zechariah 5:17 say, 'Therefore, He [who] is in Christ is a new creature. Old things are passed way. Behold all things [are] become new.'"

Similarly, an older resident of the women's halfway house described her struggle with drugs for three decades and how her "heart is different" since her recent religious conversion at the facility:

> Well, I was a junkie for 30 years. I've shot dope for 30 years straight. Wait, I've spent 3 of it in rehabs and they did not help me. They were 90-day programs. So really, I just thought this one ain't gonna help me either, but I'm gonna go to keep from going to prison. But when I got up here, boy, it was like God took over and it's totally changed me. My heart is different. My thoughts are different. If I catch little [negative] thoughts trying to creep in my mind, I get it back on what God has totally done for me. . . . God is doing a new thing in my life and every day I wake up with an expectancy of hope for my future. I never thought I could have a future. I thought I would go to my grave having to have a shot of dope every day. But I don't, and that is so awesome for me to sit here and say that cause only God knows the struggles I've been through in my life.

Another woman from the halfway house compared an average day before and after her religious conversion. After a brief moment of contemplation, she came to this conclusion:

> My bad days now is not half as bad as my good days then. It doesn't add up. I'd rather have a bad day now than to be at my best high, living it up [with] all the money and the party.

Embedded within these discussions of the old self and new self, the interviewees typically gave real-world examples or reasonable hypothetical examples of how their attitudes and behaviors had changed since conversion. It would have been easy for them to provide talking points or sound bite answers about how they had changed. In part I expected religious inmates to speak much like the average politician: with major emotion but with minor depth, but for the most part, this was not the case among those I interviewed. I asked the women at Tutwiler prison how they handled conflicts before conversion and after. Consider this response from an inmate who had been there for over a decade:

> And His whole ministry is about love and the love walk. And in order to walk in love, I have to love you regardless, like He loved me regardless. So if you come up to me and cuss me out, that does not give me the right to cuss you out. It's just not how Christianity works for me. And I'm taking myself outside of His presence and outside of my example as a Christian if I respond the same way as you do.

I was a bit skeptical of this answer, and so I pressed her a bit on this issue. I asked how she could just turn off every human impulse to respond to conflict with more conflict. This was her response:

> I've learned how to be submissive to Him in my life, in my flesh. There have been times when somebody has said something smart, or I woke up in a bad mood and somebody just look at me all lopsided and you want to say something to them. But I rebuke Satan. In my mind, I'm like, "I'm not going to fall for that. I'm not going for it this time." My body is for the Lord, and my conversation will be seasoned with salt.

This issue of the old self versus the new self among those in prisons and halfway houses will be discussed in greater detail in the coming chapters. For now the conclusion I draw is that the concept of "radical change" following religious conversion emerged with great frequency in the narratives of the 173 interviewees. How this radical change is related to identity formation, identify maintenance, and coping with confinement will be explored in Chapters 5 through 7.

## The Start of a New Journey

When describing a religious conversion, inmates often will stress the importance of it being only the first step in a lifetime journey of faith. Although the conversion is described as a life-changing event, it is only the beginning and not the end of a spiritual journey (Clear et al. 2000; Maruna, Wilson, and Curran 2006). New religious converts typically are encouraged by chaplains and local volunteers to get involved in many different religious activities. New converts also are taught that no matter how bad their lives were prior to conversion, now they have the opportunity to create positive changes. Indeed, it was evident that the prison chaplains, local religious congregants, and workers at the halfway house used the treatment modality of visualizing a new journey or new race as they worked with offenders.

One example of how the new journey is conceptualized is the "spiritual birthday" referenced commonly by women in the halfway house. The women claimed that their conversion experience restarted their lives and thus allowed them to embark on a new journey. The clear social psychological effect of this mindset was that they could distance themselves from mistakes made after their natural birth. Once they created a safe psychological distance from their negative past, the women claimed that they could focus all of their energies on maintaining a positive self following their religious conversion, or what some called their "supernatural birth."

Perhaps the most insightful description of the spiritual journey came from a women who was about two-thirds of the way through her time at the halfway house. With little prompting, she summarized where she was in her spiritual journey at the moment of the interview and how she expected the journey to unfold. Because she referred to herself in the third person with all the temerity of basketball star LeBron James, I will use the pseudonym "Leslie" in the quote below to protect her identity:

> Leslie is an awesome person of God who is not where she needs to be, but is striving to get there at a steady pace. Leslie is honest today. Leslie has integrity today. Semi-good reputation today. I am a lover of people today. I am willing today to find a different or new way. I think out processes today. I don't just jump in the boat and say let's ride when there is fifty holes and it's going to sink. I think I play that tape out. . . . Leslie is happy today, full of joy.

Another resident at the halfway house noted that in her spiritual journey there was the constant temptation to think back to all of her previous mistakes—what she called "baggage"—with drugs and crime and to feel guilty about them. However, she claimed that since her religious conversion, she tried to stay positive and to think more about the future. She summarized her journey this way:

You don't have to carry your baggage around with you forever. Some of us look back. I mean, I still do. I try not to, but I am much better about getting myself back on track and thinking that you can't go back. You just go forward. That's something that they really . . . that's a point that they continue, continue to put in you. It's a journey. You constantly strive to do better and be better day by day by day. But, if you falter along the way, you ask for forgiveness and it's okay.

Initially it seemed counterintuitive to me, but the majority of interviewees at the halfway house saw the next step in their journey as helping others in the same situation. Rather than wanting to flee the difficult and often depressing environment of a halfway house in search of new and more positive environments, the women expressed strong interest in working at a halfway house or some type of rehabilitation or counseling organization after their release. The steps in the journey, as they claimed, were simple. They started by "getting their minds right" and then "giving back" so that others from the same difficult situations could do the same. Consider this narrative of a women about to released:

I wanna go to the hospitals. I wanna go to old folks' homes. I wanna go to the schools, talk to the kids, let them know my journey and stay active in the community, and stay in church. Do all the things I allowed myself not to do, I wanna do today. You know, just stay active, go to my meetings and stay acquainted. . . . I just wanna help everybody, because somebody in my life walk, since I been on my journey, someone helped me. As a child that has always been my passion because my grandmother got put in a wheelchair and oh I just loved caring for her, you know what I'm saying? That's just my passion, it's my passion to show love and to give love. . . . Because I'm well aware of being homeless, being without, going without, and doing without. So there's nothing that another woman is going through that I haven't been through, so I just want to let the women know today that I've been there and I understand.

A second example of the new journey framework comes from the national prison ministry program Operation Starting Line (OSL). This program held a one-day event at Parchman prison in not long before I arrived to conduct my study. The program organizers hoped to start a process in which inmates committed themselves to lives of faith and to improving their relationships with other inmates, prison staff, and family members. In summarizing the purpose of the OSL event, the program organizers suggested that:

A starting line is just that—the start of a marathon run through life. Through OSL, prisoners learn to come under a new "coach"—the Lord and Savior Jesus Christ—who alone can transform their hearts and set them free from bondage to sin and crime. (*OSL* 2002)

Thus, as the name of the event implies, program organizers attempted to create a starting point from which inmates might change their attitudes and behaviors in the prison context and beyond. The OSL event was designed to begin a process (race) toward a different way of life. One male inmate who attended the event recounted how it caused him to think about the way he was running his spiritual race, as well as how other inmates were competing in the race:

If you don't have no spirituality in your life, bro, you're lost. You just running around in cycles, you hear me? You need someone else than what you been seeing. You need to get tired of running your head into the brick wall. And believe it or not, a lot of guys have really changed their life in prison and have hung with it and done good and are still doing good out there in the free world. Cause some guys really want to be helped. So I praise Him.

Another Parchman inmate reflected on the OSL event, as well as the regular religious services held in his unit:

Well, it [the religious event] gave me hope, it gave me hope. It gave me hope in the aspect of, you can still you know, you can still complete your goals and things although you've been in prison. . . . And it gave me a dedication where at the time that they came I was really feeling kind of down. And when they left that just gave me much more strength to keep on running, you know it just helped me get back in the race, and start back fighting the good fight.

Likewise, women inmates interviewed at Tutwiler prison used much of the same terminology as they described what happened following their religious conversion. The inmates were fairly evenly split in terms of their confidence in and preparation for the spiritual journey, regardless of when it began. For some there was much trepidation. When asked about her faith and the new spiritual journey, one inmate described in vivid detail her internal and external struggles:

How does it [faith] help me get through? I keeps my mind—like I ask for peace. I say, "Lord, you know sometimes attitudes flare out." I ask Him, "I need your comfort, I need your strength, I need you to give me the mind. If I need you to bridle my tongue, let the words of my mouth and the meditation of my heart be acceptable, Lord." The Lord is the strength and my redeemer. I need Him. Every step of this thing I'm going through. As I walk on this journey, I cannot step without Him. I can't. It's too much going on. I want Him to guide my tongue, everything. . . . Ever since I been here, this is what I've been doing. Drawing closer and closer to Jesus, you know. Putting off my sin. We're all of flesh, and the church helps me. The wonderful Christian fellowship, you know. It's awesome.

Other inmates seemed to approach the journey in a much more confident and optimistic manner. In their view, the race was a "gift" and the "victory was already won." Note the exuberance in this inmate's summary of her journey, especially as she repeats the last phrase three times, each time more emphatically:

[Faith] becomes a habit, like I guess you would say, waking up and lighting a cigarette first thing in the morning. It becomes a habit to sit down and say, "Ok, Lord. Let's go. Let's roll. We can do this. I'm here, you can have me. Whatever you want me to do, that's why I'm going to do it. I'm going to read my Scripture and I'm going to feed my spirit, and then hey, here we go. We're off to the races." And that's how I look at it, because if not, I may not be able to handle the things that come at me. I may not be able to handle so and so coming and cussing me out, or I may not be able to be aware of what He wants me to do that day. I've learned to take myself out of it. It's not about you. It's not about you! It's not about you!

A final dimension of the narratives on starting the new journey is the way that interviewees discussed when their new journey began. For most the journey had many stops and starts, partly due to a rough terrain, and partly due to their own "bad choices." One inmate from Parchman described the beginning of his journey at age 16, but only recently had he used the concept of a journey of faith as motivation to make positive changes in his life. He claimed that he "backslid" during his early adult life, and had to "get back in the race" after he went to prison:

At [the] age of 16, I was baptized. From that point, I have always— [the Bible] states that the beginning of knowledge is the fear [of] God—and from that point I've always feared God because there was a question asked me and fear come on me. The question was: "If you died today what would you, would you know if you were going to heaven or hell?" The question feared me, and looking back on it, that was the beginning of the fear for me, really fearing God.

An elderly male inmate who wondered if he was too old to start a new journey described his experience:

> I decided to give my life to the Lord. I committed myself to it and Mr. X had told us one time, when he was talking and he told us when you give your life to the Lord it's not gonna be like . . . the Lord He still knows where we are, you know. The only difference that's gonna be is that you gonna be a Christian in bondage [prison] and the Lord is going to provide for you. He will take care of you and he gave us some assurance. He gave me some. [Mr. X] said "Just go ahead on. You probably don't want to get saved because you in prison. You don't want to give your life to the Lord because you think something might happen or the wrong thing might happen. People won't give you the respect." He took a little more time with me, explaining to me to go on and surrender, just give God a chance, you know. With the little time I have left, give God a chance. You know, so I did that.

This narrative is fairly remarkable given what we know about how older inmates and those with lengthy sentences generally prefer to "do their time." They tend to settle into predictable patterns and typically do not take many risks. This inmate, however, was determined to start a journey of faith with the "little time" he had left in life.

## Summary

The narrative of the jailhouse convert is a common one, and one that arouses much suspicion. From the most active member of a local faith congregation to the most ardent atheist or agnostic, there is strong skepticism of religious conversions reported from prison settings, in particular when high-profile or violent offenders are involved. Maruna, Wilson, and Curran (2006, p. 162) provide an insightful summary of this skepticism surrounding jailhouse converts:

> Prisoners who "find religion" are thought to be most likely putting on an act to impress parole boards, win plum assignments in the prison (e.g., working with the chaplain), or gain public sympathy. The radical nature of the transformation they describe appears to violate our assumptions about the way individuals change. Finding God behind bars seems somehow too convenient to be believable.

Yet for all of the common conceptions of religious conversion among those in correctional contexts, very little academic research on the topic has been done. My contention is that prisons and halfway houses are, in fact, ideal settings for understanding the process of religious conversion. In that sense I am in agreement with Maruna, Wilson, and Curran (2006, p. 163), who argued for the study of religious converts in the "extreme" environment of prison by noting that "the prison provides a stark and vivid social context for exploring the conditions that allow for quantum personality change. The prison can be understood as one of the social contexts in which self-identity is most likely to be questioned."

In this chapter I went beyond simplistic preoccupations with whether the claims of religious conversion among the incarcerated are "real." Instead, I moved the conversation forward by exploring the claims made about prison conversions by the captives themselves, the specific context in which conversions occur, and what the conversion experiences mean to them. Based on my analysis of 173 in-depth interviews, four important themes emerged: (1) the timing of conversion, (2) the emotions of conversion, (3) a new faith-based identity, and (4) the start of a new journey.

What is most fascinating from my perspective is that the interviewees claimed that their extreme emotional shift occurred in only the time it took them to sense a need for a higher power, confess wrongdoing, and commit to a relationship with that higher power. I also observed that most of the reported conversions occurred while the interviewees were in prison or a halfway house, and occurred in the midst of major troubles and low points in their lives, or what most called "rock bottom." From the analysis it was evident that the majority of the conversions had all of the crisis and drama of Saul's famous conversion as recorded in Scriptures, but without the bright lights, temporary blindness, and audible voice of God.

Finally, in terms of social psychological impact, I found that the religious conversions allowed the prisoners, despite their many past mistakes, to portray themselves as being in control of their current and future lives. They reinterpreted their past not as "wasted time" but as part of a "spiritual journey." This gave them a greater appreciation for and focus on the present part of the journey (Clear et al. 2000; Maruna 2001; Maruna, Wilson, and Curran 2006). Although the converts may still excuse their past transgressions because of "uncontrollable forces," their new, faith-based identities allow them to discover a "new self" or even a "true self" (Maruna, Wilson, and Curran 2006). Now armed with a more thorough understanding of religious conversion among those in prisons and halfway houses, I move on to consider how faith impacts the ability of inmates to cope with the extreme difficulties of prison life.

# 5

# Maintaining Change for Men

In the previous chapter I explored the issue of religious conversion among prison inmates. In this chapter I continue the story and explore how male inmates live that faith while in prison. To be sure, maintaining religious commitment appears to be extremely difficult. The gap between faith and behavior is often a wide one. From decades of research among members of the general public, we know that at least 90 percent of Americans say that they believe in a higher power and yet only about 25–30 percent can be categorized as regular attenders in local religious congregations. (Regular attendance typically is defined as one or more times per week.) An even smaller percentage donates money (a tithe) to their local congregation (Sherkat and Ellison 1999).

This being the case for those in free society, it is not uncommon for the incarcerated to have a religious conversion but eventually to "backslide." This concept means that their level of religious commitment may be diminished over time and they may resort to their "prior selves" (Maruna 2001). Despite the best intentions or motivations of inmates, their conversion may become less salient over time and may fail to create prosocial behaviors. Kerley, Matthews, and Schulz (2005), for example, found that 94 percent of inmates reported belief in a higher power, but only about 39 percent attended weekly religious services.

Much of the decline in religious commitment can be attributed to the nature of prison life. Not surprisingly, there is widespread consensus among researchers and former inmates that prisons are dark and dehumanizing places. Several notable researchers have gone to great lengths to describe the deprivation, isolation, questionable rules, unethical correctional officers, and conflicts that are central to prison life (Irwin 1985; Johnson and Toch 1982; Sykes 1958). Clear and his colleagues assert that the most painful feature of prison life, simply, is the loss of freedom: "Whatever else the prison does, it makes the inmate stay in a place he would not choose" (Clear et al. 2000, p. 62).

**Prison Coping and the Role of Faith**

Given the unparalleled increase in incarceration rates over the past 40 years and the dehumanizing context of prison life, it follows that researchers have explored how inmates are able to cope. I contend that understanding how inmates cope with prison life is important not only for the health and safety of inmates, but also for the protection of correctional personnel. Research on prison coping often takes one of three forms. First, early researchers focused on identifying specific stressors that inmates might encounter while in prison (Johnson and Toch 1982; Sykes 1958). Second, other researchers studied prison coping in terms of inmate classification and the creation of treatment programs (Wooldredge 1999; Wright 1989). Third, another group of researchers explored variations in inmates' coping ability and the specific resources that inmates use to cope.

This body of research indicates that many individual and institutional factors impact the ability of inmates to cope—both in terms of emotions and behavior—with prison life. At the individual level, factors such as age, educational attainment, criminal history, sentence length, and psychopathology are all strong predictors of prison adjustment and coping (MacKenzie 1987; MacKenzie and Goodstein 1985; Warren et al. 2004). Institutional factors associated with prison coping include inmates' control of prison environment, time served, level of crowding, and limited resources (MacKenzie, Goodstein, and Blouin 1987; MacKenzie, Robinson, and Campbell 1989).

Nearly all of the early prison-coping studies failed to devote much attention to the role that religious faith and practice might play. At the same time there was an impressive literature developing on how faith could be used to cope with a wide array of stressful life events among those in the free world. Probably the most comprehensive work was Pargament's (1997) *The Psychology of Religion and Coping*. Using several different datasets and methodologies, Pargament concluded that religion can serve as a positive coping mechanism for individuals dealing with diverse adverse situations such as divorce, unemployment, depression, illness, loss of loved ones, and war.

Inspired in part by Pargament's work, previously I explored the topic of religion and coping among prison inmates. I conducted the first representative survey of inmates about religious attitudes and behaviors, and did so in one of the largest prison facilities in the southern region. My colleagues and I wanted to explore the degree to which religiosity impacted emotional and behavioral forms of prison coping. Although we found that those with greater levels of religious commitment were less likely to get into arguments and fights, we did not find any differences when we examined the presence and extent of negative emotions among inmates (Kerley, Matthews, and Blanchard 2005; Kerley, Allison, and Graham 2006). In short, religious inmates were no less depressed, sad, angry, or bitter than moderately or nonreligious inmates. At first these conclusions were a bit perplexing. Why would religious faith help inmates tone down negative behaviors, but not tone down negative emotions? After careful thought and review of the literature, we reached the conclusion that it must be a byproduct of the prison context. This was our conclusion at the time:

> The nature of the prison context may be a root cause for the differential effects of religiosity on prison coping. As noted previously, prisons are dehumanizing places that strip individuals of freedom, dignity, and identity. We contend that prison life is emotionally debilitating to the point that religion does not seem to significantly reduce the experience of negative emotions. Yet religion does appear to structure interpersonal relationships in prison positively by reducing negative interactions that could escalate to more serious interpersonal conflict. Thus, even though religion may not be able to significantly reduce the inward feeling of negative emotions, it does appear to impact the quality of interpersonal relationships. (Kerley, Allison, and Graham 2006, p. 87)

All of this setup leads to this key question: what makes some religious converts better able to cope with prison life than others? Having documented change that occurs from religious conversions in the previous chapter, it is equally important to understand change that is maintained while incarcerated.

As described in the Appendix, 63 in-depth interviews were conducted at Mississippi State Penitentiary in Parchman, Mississippi. Located deep in the Mississippi Delta region, Parchman, as it is commonly called, is the largest of Mississippi's three state-managed facilities and is one of the largest prisons in the nation in terms of acreage and inmate population. Inmates interviewed were actively involved in at least one religious program at the prison. At the time of the study, there were three types of religious programs in which minimum- and medium-security inmates could participate. Participants for the in-depth interviews were recruited by staff chaplains at the facility. A total of 63 interviews were conducted over a 12-month period.

The purpose of the interviews was to investigate inmates' religiosity and how this affected their self-images, ability to cope with incarceration, and incidence of prosocial and antisocial behavior. Each interview began with a discussion of inmates' family and religious backgrounds. Inmates were then asked to trace the impact of religion on their lives to their present situation, and asked to describe the experience of being incarcerated and adjusting to the prison context. Next, I asked how they were able to create and maintain faith-based identities in the prison context. Finally, inmates were asked about the experience of negative emotions and the negative behaviors in which they may have engaged.

Overall, inmates interviewed for this study recognized that a religious conversion—whether it occurred before or since their current period of incarceration—was critical in empowering them to deal with prison life. However, they emphasized that they needed to remain committed to their faith if they were to cope effectively with the harsh conditions of incarceration. They also claimed that their religious commitment provided them with a clear way to reinterpret their current living situation, to have some measure of control over it, and to have a greater sense of purpose.

This theme is similar to one found by Maruna, Wilson, and Curran (2006) in their study of 75 inmates. Incarceration typically is accompanied not only by physical isolation, but also emotional isolation. Inmates almost immediately can experience a loss of all purpose and control in their lives, and their identities are reshaped accordingly. A religious conversion may interrupt that process, and then restart it from the perspective of a relationship with a higher power and a new "divine purpose." The investigators summarized it this way:

> Religious conversion can help relieve a sense of psychological crisis because it can provide meaning in the face of meaningless and identity integration when confronted with circumstances that cause individuals to question their sense of identity. . . . In spite of their painful experiences in prison, almost all of the interviewees were now able to recast their imprisonment not as a personal crisis, but as a gift or opportunity. (Maruna, Wilson, and Curran 2006, p. 175)

The inmates in my study described in vivid details the struggles of prison life such as inconsistent rules and regulations, threats to safety, poor living conditions, and inadequate health care. They claimed that religion could help them to reinterpret their current situation, and more effectively manage the negative emotions that are so commonplace in prison life. The inmates did not claim that their religious conversion was a panacea for all of their ills, nor did they believe that the prison was instantaneously more livable following the conversion. They did, however, believe that they could effectively minimize the negative emotional consequences of prison life through faith.

## Separating the Wheat from the Chaff

The first pervasive theme to emerge from the inmate narratives was the importance of associating with the right people. As is typical in evangelical religious traditions, the inmates interviewed placed a strong focus on surrounding themselves with religious others. They claimed that if they could surround themselves with other "saints," both inside and outside of prison, they would be less likely to falter. They also discussed their desires and attempts to rekindle dampened relations and to develop new ones with like-minded others who could provide positive support and encouragement. This is reflected in how one inmate described a relative who helped him understand how he could be in prison and yet still have an important purpose in life:

> When I first became incarcerated, my mother was, she did what a mother would do, came to the rescue. We wrote a lot and I had a Godmother, she used to write me a lot and she used to always encourage me with Scriptures and the Bible and you know tellin' me that, you know, keep my head up and that some of God's greatest men were in prison and stuff like that. So I did go through that phase where I had family members that was being there. God blessed me with a wife and she's been there every step of the way.

Nearly all of the inmates described everyday life in prison as an inner struggle between "godly" and "worldly" influences. They asserted that it was difficult to stay on the side of the godly because the temptations in prison were widespread and overwhelming at times. They believed that it was important as part of their new or renewed faith commitment to avoid temptations, and nearly all of them described their main goal in prison as being able to "stay on the right track." In most settings maintaining a new outlook on life takes deliberate effort, and perhaps this is even more the case in prison. To be successful, inmates claimed that they had to be diligent about their new faith-based identities, or else they would easily be consumed by the negativity of prison life. To stay positive, they needed strong ties to prosocial people on a regular basis.

Inmates frequently described how their new faith-based outlook allowed them to have similar interpretations of the world as their loved ones, and thus allowed them to better connect and to communicate. In describing an improved relationship with his wife, one inmate stated:

> The religious program, it really helped me out. It really made me and my wife more connected because by her being on a religious level, and I wasn't on a religious level, and she was coming to me all the time, so now I understand where she coming from.

Another inmate described how his family connections provided inspiration to be hopeful, especially during the most difficult emotional times:

> But, even though being incarcerated, my family was a large inspiration, still because my grandmother, she never failed to write. But, she would write me every week and would tell me: "God's gonna make a way, God's gonna make a way, you know. Hold on." Even at times it look like I'm at my weakest point. And then my Mom would write me.

Many inmates described the importance of developing friendships with other religious individuals. Although most inmates had positive friends on the outside, the majority of the narratives describe supportive friendships that were forged while they were in prison:

> The ministers, they gave us some addresses to write to them, you know, and they'll send us some Bible Scriptures and stuff like that, where we can keep ourselves going on with the Lord. My preacher out there in the world, he be keeping in contact with me. And I write him, and you know, they be keeping me up, you know, going on to church and everything, and my friends been writing me, calling me, talking to me and everything. They're a real special part of my life. If it wasn't for them, I don't think I could make it.

Another inmate described a supportive relationship with an inmate from another facility and his mother:

> I have a friend, me and him met in another facility. Me and him had got cool, we even got into drugs, shoot ball and stuff together, but you know, I got saved, and like about two months later he got saved and so, you know, I met his mom, and she been there, she really like been a mom to me. And, you know, me and him always just been real with one another. That's what make it easier when you got somebody who you can trust. Then, since I've been saved, and met brothers who are serious about serving God, and you know that understand being saved

and in this prison here. You know you have someone who on the same page you on. Makes it easier, you know?

What started as one very negative friendship involving illicit drug use was transformed over time into two positive friendships. The inmate attributed the positive relationships to a new faith commitment, and noted how they helped him to cope with the loneliness of prison life.

Perhaps the most remarkable story was of the positive connection between an inmate who was an evangelical Christian and another inmate from the Muslim faith. In a connection reminiscent of the unlikely pairing of Andy Dufresne and Red from the movie *Shawshank Redemption*, these inmates developed plans to continue their friendship after release. In particular, the inmate I interviewed described the hope that this friendship provided him:

> Just like I was saying about my friend that is a Muslim, he gets out nine months before I do and . . . I correspond with his mother and father too on religious matters. He basically told me, "When I get out, you know where you going?" I said, "Where?" He said "You are going to go with me or I'm going to get you to come up there where I'm at, and that is where you're going to be." He said, "You don't have nothing down here and you don't have no reason to go anywhere else." And it's hope. He has given me hope to look forward to something, even though it is 12 years down the road. So, he gives me hope and I have to look at him and see God in him too. Because that is the only way we can see Jesus is through other people.

It is clear that supportive relationships are crucial in allowing inmates to make it, but the inmates claimed that the most important newly forged relationships were those that also took on a mentoring quality. The people they made these connections with varied in terms of their positions in the prison, often including members of the prison's correctional staff. One inmate told the story of a correctional officer who made a major impact:

> She was an officer up here. You know, she always pushed me. Tried to push me to the limit. She'd make me go to school every day and every time I'd come back from school she'd have me some work to do. I used to help her and she used to help show me how to do gardening and stuff like that, and digging flowerbeds. When I would miss school she would say: "You know you got to get your GED now. That's what you coming for." She pushed me so hard until I finally got it. If it wouldn't of been for her, I don't think I would of made it this far.

Another inmate described his relationship with a volunteer from a drug treatment program operated in the facility:

> When I first got here there was this young lady that I met in Narcotics Anonymous, and I can say she was a true friend. And, since I've been here, she writes me, and we talk about God, and we talk about the program Narcotics Anonymous, and, you know it's been a big help for me, just to have somebody out there, like her to write me. You know, it seems like at times, I would get a letter from her, and it would be at a time when I was at one of my lowest points. And, her letter would just pick me right up because something, one little specific thing that she said in the letter it was like she knew, that I was down at that time.

Besides making efforts to connect with positive religious others, the inmates were also aware of the need to avoid all sorts of negative influences. The inmates were well aware of the ubiquitous temptations of prison life. The avoidance of temptation is a challenging task for all inmates, but one that must be made if they are to stay focused and to retain their new faith-based identities. Nearly every inmate discussed the importance of "staying on the right track" or a similar mantra. They claimed that their faith provided them with the motivation to stay on the right track while dealing with the struggles of day-to-day prison life. One inmate described his struggle to avoid negative situations this way:

> Well, at first, when I first came here, you know, um, I really didn't want to get too religious, because you know, I didn't want, I guess it was my pride. I didn't want folks thinking, "Well, because you in an organization, this right here you know, you changing on us." But then I had to look at it that I'm doing this time myself and the only way I can do it is by having God in my life, so I had to back away from everything else to have my religion.

Perhaps the most striking idea to emerge from the avoidance strategies was that inmates referred to negative influences in the abstract. For the most part the inmates did not pinpoint specific negative individuals. The expression, "If you lie with dogs, you'll get fleas"—or one similar—was a common one in this prison setting, but just who the "dogs" are remains unclear. This is in stark contrast to the description of positive relations discussed previously where the inmates frequently mentioned by name the positive individuals with whom they attempted to interact. When they mentioned avoiding negative people it was usually with expressions like "gang members" or "young guns" and included anyone who caused "trouble." The religious inmates recognized that nothing good would come from spending time with troublemakers, and so they made efforts to physically and emotionally separate themselves from those individuals. One inmate described his struggles and the changes he was forced to make in his associates:

> Well, since coming to Parchman, I've had to change the folks I hang with cause the folks I hang with, they mostly run around with gangs, you know, they in gangs. So, I had to change and start hanging with some Christian brothers. Somebody trying to get their life straightened, you know, trying to serve the Lord too. So for me to do that, I had to tell them, "Well, I'll have to leave y'all alone." So I had to just break my way and just start hanging with Christian brothers, just start prayin' and servin' in my unit, you know. And, that's the way it's been since then.

Another inmate described a similar situation:

> Any type of thing that'll cause a problem, you know, you kind of stay away from it. If you're out in the zone, you're arguing all the time, and you start getting into the word because you don't want to fight, you don't want to hurt nobody, you know. The only way you going to not do that, is leave that alone and start doing Christ-like things. You'd be surprised the people that you help just by them seeing you done turned your life around.

To remain resolute in their new faith commitments, it was necessary to make good decisions concerning their associates. When choosing with whom to interact, religious inmates claimed that their faith would help them to make those good decisions. However, they were quick to acknowledge that they are not perfect and cannot make the right decisions every time. One older inmate who had been in prison for over two decades provided a simple formula for making good decisions about people he should spend time with:

> [Faith] keeps you from going and doing, like you might want to go hang with these guys but you know they are trouble. You know that if they do something they gonna get you too because they are trouble and you were seen with them. So, I feel like you reading the Bible and praying that gonna keep you from going the wrong way and running with them. Unless you trying to share the word with them and show them that this is the right way. Other than that, you not gonna be messing with them. I feel like from reading the Bible and praying, you gonna fall off sometime on the wrong side, but it gonna hit you, you're not supposed to be there. If you're not reading the Bible and praying, then what you doing may be negative.

Another inmate described how he joined a gang early during his prison stint, but then left it when he made a commitment to faith:

> Well, at that time, the one time when I first came to Parchman, I was on the negative activities. I was associating with organizations. And as I got older and got wiser and acknowledged that I was lost and started drawing unto God and God started drawing unto me, I had to sacrifice, I had to let the organizations go, and put Christ and serve him with the full perfection through salvation. That's where I'm at now. I have to sacrifice by resigning from the organizations that I was in. I gave it up to be redeemed for Christ 'cause I felt God had laid on my heart that I couldn't serve two masters. I had to love one and hate the other one.

Thus, the inmates made it clear that they attempted to form positive relationships with people, both inside and outside prison, once they established a new faith-based identity. If successful in creating those relationships, the inmates would have something to which they could look forward. Whether it was a simple conversation with a fellow inmate or local volunteer, or perhaps an uplifting letter from home, they believed that those interactions often were the metaphorical kindling they needed to keep the fires of their conversion burning. On the other hand, the 63 inmates I interviewed claimed that avoiding negative others was just as important as connecting with positive others. The inmates claimed that they were constantly struggling with temptations and thus needed to use their faith to make good decisions on a daily basis.

## Private Practice

Now I turn to the specific religious practices used by the inmates to help them cope with the difficulties of incarceration. The first approach is to engage in what I will call the "private practice" of faith. I recognize that perhaps nothing truly can be private in a prison setting, but the idea is that some religious behaviors are meant to be personal and solo efforts. In what was the most striking development from my analysis of the 63 transcripts, the inmates seemed to place less emphasis on the private practice of faith as compared to the "public practice" of faith, which will be discussed in the next section.

### Prayer

Nearly all of the inmates noted the need for personal prayer on a daily basis, and about 75 percent reported that they did pray at least once per day. Personal prayer or meditation is a fascinating religious ritual, and one that is crucial to nearly all of the major world religions. Most religions encourage their adherents to set aside time each day for prayer and meditation, but the extent to which this religious activity is formalized varies. Some religions outline specific guidelines for prayer such as the number of times per day, the time of day, the location of prayer, and the position of the body. In other religions, adherents are taught to be more in a constant mindset of prayer that resembles a running conversation with a higher power. Regardless of the technique, the clear idea is that this religious activity is meant to keep a person's thoughts focused on spiritual matters, and to maintain a strong connection with a higher power.

The descriptions of prayer from the inmates centered around several key issues. Inmates stressed the importance of having times of prayer daily, or at least on a regular basis. Consistency was considered the most crucial aspect of the prayer experience, as evidenced in this quote:

> You know, I [pray] every day. Me and God have a one-on-one. I talk with Him, I pray, it's just something that I've growed up to do.

One inmate who had been involved in religious services for several years explained his need for daily prayer time:

> Well I do it on a daily basis, try to keep it up, try to maintain it because it is really important to me and you know without any fellowship in my life with the Lord, you know, I have no peace I have no settledness. It's always like a stormy sea in a sense and I feel that that is very important to me and for anybody else as well because that is what you really want to do is just maintain your fellowship with the Lord and it's been a great experience. I love it.

Another inmate described how consistency in prayer created in him a sense of optimism, as well as a surprisingly sanguine view of having spent over a decade in the prison facility:

> I do [pray] every morning and evening before I go to bed every night. I thank the Lord for watching over me and blessing me throughout this day. Blessing me to allow me to be here and lay back down. Like in the morning, I thank him for waking me up. You know I tell the officers here that I am blessed. But next month will make 11 years that I've done been here at Parchman, and I done been here and I'm in good shape and health.

As the inmates became consistent in the religious ritual of prayer, they often reported increased levels of emotional and even physical support. In fact, they tended to dislike the term "ritual," and instead reframed prayer as an "experience." The benefits of prayer outlined by the inmates included inspiration, strength, rejuvenation, peace, and contentment. One inmate who admitted years of struggles with inadequacy and vulnerability explained how prayer made him feel strong enough to face the challenges of prison life:

> Well, [prayer] done helped build my inner strength. I know prayer have helped, you know what I'm saying. I know to ask God. I've experienced a few so I know there's a God, and I've asked him to help me, you know, walk with me, you know, you know guide me every day, you know to work on all the things I have problems with.

One inmate who had been in prison for less than one year for a nonviolent offense described being terrified as he entered the facility because of the potential to be harmed by others. Even the thought of interacting with violent offenders caused anxiety. However, he claimed that prayer helped him to adjust to the facility and turned his outlook on prison from "dreadful" to "brightful:"

> I prayed, because when I first made it to Parchman, I was scared. I was scared because a lot of folks here around me you know they was here for life, murders, and stuff like that. I just pray because I didn't know what was going to happen, you know, what was going to happen in the next two or three years or later on cause it was just, I was outnumbered. I don't know nobody up here at the time, but once I got going around absolutely praying, asking the Lord for protection, guiding, everything just you know it opened my past whatever, focused, so you know everything got brightful it sure did.

Another inmate who claimed to be dealing with major episodes of depression described the value of prayer for him:

> [When] I'm down and out and I lay and dwell on it a while and this sad feelings come over me, so I just kneel down and pray to God. Pray to God, you know, God, he hold all this power in his hands, so you know, God he has the power to give me joy, peace, and happiness and I've experienced this whole world, this whole evil world that you know, no one really that you can trust. Not even your family, but God tell you that he never leave, he never forsake you, he's always there when you need him, regardless of what the situation is. So, it makes me feel good just to know, just to call upon him and know He's my pride, you know.

The inmates suggested that as they matured in their faith, it was essential that they spend even more time in prayer so that they could face the challenges of prison with a "full tank." Interestingly, the inmates argued that the closer they became to God, the more they sensed all sorts of temptations in their lives. One inmate who described himself as "quick tempered" claimed that his prayer time had a major calming effect when he was tempted to say or do things that might lead to a rules violation report (i.e., the term used in this prison facility for disciplinary infractions):

> Faith makes things better because you want to be left alone for a moment to pray. It is good to be alone sometimes, because you can get where you can pray all the time, cry if you want to, talk to God and it's good. Like I say it's good for the implosive energy you have inside because you might be explosive and you might act like a fool. I've seen guys like that so it's better to talk to God and have faith.

## Scripture Reading and Study

The second example of private religious practice involved the reading of Scriptures or sacred texts by the inmates. Having come from traditions of evangelical Protestant faith, their book of choice was the Bible, although they often read accompanying books or commentaries. Overall, the inmates' descriptions of Scripture study closely mirrored those of prayer time in terms of the purpose and benefits. The focus on consistency in reading was an important part of the narratives. Most of the inmates described a fairly regimented schedule in which they would read at certain times of the day and for certain lengths of time. One inmate who was assigned to the dreaded first breakfast shift at 5:00 A.M. described his routine:

> I have a daily devotion to the Lord. I have a daily reading in the morning. This is when I get my best reading, at like 4 o'clock in the morning. When, pretty much, a lot of people are still asleep. Sometime the Lord will wake me up and I just grab my Bible and I'll read and pray and meditate upon that day. And I read throughout the day, whenever I get a chance. . . . I try to read Scriptures throughout the day, some Psalms or some Proverbs. You know, try to just keep myself fed with spiritual food. You know, it helps me, it helps me. This is the freest I've ever felt.

The inmates described a spiritual imperative to read Scriptures daily that was so strong, apparently it could cause stress and guilt when they failed to do so. One inmate expressed his frustration with finding uninterrupted times to read:

> As soon as you set down on your rack, a dude is wanting to come and kick it with you. You got a lot of people who don't respect the fact that you got your Bible out and will wait and come back in a minute. They just sit down and act like it ain't never been open. If you can ever get the time or are able to sit down by yourself, [Scripture reading] helps a lot.

In terms of what is to be gained by the routine reading and study of Scriptures, the inmates described a wide variety of benefits. One longtime inmate commented:

> Reading the word of God is really inspiring to me all of the time, because there's something about it always new to you, you know. It's great.

Thus, even as they read many of the same passages repeatedly, most inmates claimed that they found new inspiration and meaning. Many inmates described their reading time with metaphors relating to food or to fuel:

> I've found that when I get burdened sometimes I pick up this book and go to reading these Scriptures and for some reason God will talk to your heart. . . . It fills you back up and you can run that race a little bit longer until you go back down and fill back up. It's like a gas tank. Gotta just keep filling it back up.

In terms of the benefits to their emotional state, many inmates described the "peace" or "peaceful mood" that would occur directly after reading Scriptures. After being pressed by the interviewer to explain in more detail what this meant, one inmate explained it this way:

> *Respondent*: It would make it more easier cause I know if I sit up and read my Bible, I, once I finish reading my Bible, I feel better, you know what I'm saying, feel better. So it's like you be in a peaceful mood, you know what I'm saying?
>
> *Interviewer*: No. What is it about that [prayer] makes you feel better?
>
> *Respondent*: It just, I guess, I don't know what it is but now I just feel, it's like some type of vibe or something come over, you know what I'm saying? Once I finish reading, I can walk around and just like I

feel good about everything. Now on down the road, I be back the same way. I'm mad, I probably need to start reading it more.

Another inmate who struggled with anxiety quoted Scriptures about "peace" in explaining why he thought that regular reading was important. When asked how he dealt with pressure situations, he gave this explanation:

> There were Scriptures and things I had to learn to calmly repeat in my mind and in my head and even when I laid down at night, you know. As Psalms if I'm not mistaken, Psalms 4:4, it will let us know, "He will lay me down in perfect peace, sweet peace, sweet sleep and perfect peace, you know and I will awake for the Lord will sustain me." You see? And Scriptures like this right here, you know, living in a hostile environment. They comforted me.

In what was perhaps the most fascinating narrative in this section, one middle-aged inmate who admitted being unable to read for his entire life explained how his desire to read Scriptures led him to take taking GED courses at the facility. After learning to read during the GED courses, he claimed that he started reading Scriptures because of his new faith commitment and so that he could practice his new reading skill:

> I read daily. If I ain't at work, 9 times out of 10 times I'm layin' up on the rack readin' that Bible. I'm gonna tell you, when I first come here, I couldn't read or write a lick and I got in that Bible and God He gonna let you read that word, ain't no doubt. I can't write real good, but I can read now. Thank God for that.

## Public Practice

Even though times of prayer and Scripture study are conceptualized as times to "get away" from others and to escape temporarily the "pains of imprisonment," from the majority of the narratives it appears that even the private practice of faith has a strong social component. One inmate provided the most cogent summary of the link between private practice and public practice:

> I can sit here and pray for somebody, but I want to go to a church. Whether it be here or wherever. I enjoy it because two or more are gathered and He blesses it. The way I look at it, He hears individuals, but I also believe He hears a congregation more. There is strength in numbers.

Thus, even for what most would consider intensely personal and private religious activities—such as prayer and Scripture study—about 70 percent of the narratives point to the social support mechanisms of religion as the root of coping successfully with confinement.

### Group Religious Services and Small Groups

Despite the perceived value of private time spent in prayer and Scripture study, it was clear that the inmates' preferred method of spiritual development and maturation involved social groups. As they attempted to maximize their contact with positive people and to remain focused and inspired about their religious beliefs, the inmates believed that the group religious activities were the most important resources they had to cope with confinement and to battle temptations. They stressed the need for chapel services (the chapel at this facility was called the Spiritual Life Center), group Scripture study, group prayer, and group discussions about religion. In their narratives of group religious practice, the inmates commonly referenced a scriptural imperative from the New Testament works of the Apostle Paul to attend religious services. The Scriptures, which several of the inmates could quote verbatim, outline an obligation of religious adherents to spend time in both formal and informal group meetings. This time with other "believers" is thought to provide encouragement, to facilitate learning about faith and scriptural texts, and to create accountability structures for attitudes, language, and behavior.

As I dug deeper in the interviews about private versus public religion, it became apparent that the conversion experience alone was not sufficient to bring about lasting positive changes to the inmates' attitudes and behavior. About 70 percent of the inmates claimed that they could not survive prison without the religious social support of others. They argued that this social support was necessary to "keep on the right track." By this they meant that they relied on social support mechanisms to keep themselves focused on and inspired by their faith. One inmate described how even his private time of Scripture reading had a necessary social dimension:

> I kind of cooled off the religious talking until nighttime at 10:00. That's the only thing I had left but my mother, that's what time she reads. . . . 10:00 we had this thing, you know, that I call her on Tuesdays and Fridays every week and . . . at 10:00 she gonna read the Bible every night you know. So I read it every night, and we kind of be like a community, although I'm here and she there.

Although he assigned value to Scripture reading, it seemed clear that likely he would not continue this ritual were it not for the social support of his mother.

Many inmates noted some of the inherent challenges of reading and understanding Scriptures such as complicated theological issues, use of literal stories versus imagery, and difficult language used in some translations. One inmate, who was particularly frustrated by reading Scriptures alone, claimed that he began going to group religious services for clarification:

> I was beatin' my head against a brick wall trying to figure something out in the Bible and I didn't really have anyone to talk to, cause like I said the chaplain here is a very busy man. And I had just started to talk to my rack partner about it that week sometime . . . and we went to one of the visiting church ministries and their little pastor that was there . . . he got on the same subject I was on and clarified some things I was having some problems with. So that helps a lot. And whether it was a human individual or the Holy Spirit, I'm not sure which, but somebody had a hand in figuring that out for me.

Another inmate expressed a similar frustration with some passages and explained that he consulted several religious inmates in his unit: "'Cause like some things I don't really just understand the Bible, [so] I go to another one of the guys I know studying the Bible and he'll help me out a little bit on that."

As they began to mature in their faith via the religious activities, the inmates claimed that it made their private practice more meaningful. That being said, the interviewees made it clear that the group context indeed was the root of their spiritual development. Not only did the inmates report inspiration from the religious activities, but also they reported how the activities inspired them to be uplifting to others and to avoid many of the pitfalls of prison. Note how this inmate described being on a spiritual level more during the group activities than during his private times of prayer and Scripture reading:

> I always took my problems to God, you know, so always, I was always on a spiritual level all the time, but you know like I say when I go to a program and when they talking about God you know, it really uplift me. Because you know [it is] the words of fellowship from another. It was a good fellowship time, you know. Like I say, when I go to church, you know, I feel good about it, so it made me feel good.

Another inmate described how the religious activities helped his emotions when he was struggling:

> And it gave me a dedication where at the time that they came I was really feeling kind of down. And when they left that just gave me much more strength to keep on running, you know it just helped me get back in the race, and start back fighting the good fight.

In what was the most alarming comment, another inmate described how the religious activities may have facilitated not just his figurative survival, but also his literal survival in prison:

> Personally, the way my personal life has changed it's I've went from I've noticed myself and my friend—I talk to once a week on the phone he's noticed it too—I don't laugh as much as I used to. I mean, there's various reasons for that. One of them is being locked up, but the other one—like I said I've lost some family members since I've been locked up and my marriage is probably heading out the door too—so if it weren't for some of the religious services around here, I would've probably either done something I didn't like to myself or either put myself in a situation where someone would do it for me, you know. Which isn't hard around here. It isn't hard at all.

In terms of spiritual maturation, many inmates described how the religious activities helped in that regard. One inmate explained how interactions in small groups helped him mature from a spiritual "baby" to a more mature person of faith:

> As I began to really understand the Bible, how things worked in here, how things goes and also at the time I was continuing read my Bible and continuing fellowshipping with the Lord and I met some guys and we talked and you know, [we] just pretend you're all in a group. It's sort of like just growing up like a child, you know, you need someone to lead you. The world may seem strange to a baby when they first come in, but you know as time goes on you began to be more familiar with a lot of things.

This inmate uses the same metaphor of maturing from a child to an adult in terms of his faith:

> Like I said I have been growing up in religion, but when I first got started it was like a new beginner of Christian. I read my Bible [but] I really didn't fully start. . . . They say you suppose to change when you become a Christian, but I really didn't start notice the change until I joined the ministry called Kairos. Kairos has changed me a lot. It has

showed me how to love somebody, godly love and everything. . . . I started getting on psychic medication [for depression] and since I joined [the religious services], I have gotten off of psychic medication. So, it has helped me a lot and showed me how to fellowship with my other Christian brothers and stuff.

It is important to note that this inmate reported reading Scriptures by himself, but claimed that he did not begin to see any spiritual development or maturation until he joined a religious program.

Another important theme to emerge from the narratives was that the inmates often described the benefits of public practice using language that reflected their experiences from the streets. For example, they often described the religious services as "parties" and the accompanying feelings or emotions as psychic "highs." Although some conservative Protestants might snarl at this approach, perhaps it is easier for the inmates to stay motivated in their faith when new highs can replace their former experiences with what Shover (1996) has called "life as party." One of the self-described deacons from the prison chapel summarized the typical religious service:

[The religious services] are joyous. It gave us something to think about. Everything that was done it was done under Christianity. It was not something that you could go down to the club and do. It was a party where there ain't nobody shooting at nobody, nobody cutting at nobody, it was a party where there wasn't nobody sick, nobody shooting no dope, smoking no dope. It was a party where they was a givin' them a gift from God. Everything that came up at those moments and those particular times, it was joy. You can't find that nowhere else unless you get with this lifestyle.

Another inmate who was serving time for a drug-related crime compared the highs he experienced as a drug user with the highs he experienced in the religious services. Here he describes an event called *Operation Starting Line* (a national program created by Prison Fellowship Ministries) that came to the prison a few months before the interview:

After the service, I stayed high up on the Lord, you know. It's just like me smoking marijuana back in the day. I was high up on the Lord that day. So, there was no negative things about that event, that day. I stayed positive all that day, and from then on, I've been lifted up. I was just depending on the Lord.

The inmates also stressed the importance of both formal and informal religious activities. The inmates interviewed were able to attend formal weekly religious services at the Spiritual Life Center, as well as small Scripture study groups conducted by the chaplains once or twice per month. In addition to these services, the inmates were also involved in Scripture study and prayer groups in their units. Many of those interviewed described how the large formal services sparked an interest in developing small informal study groups:

> Well, after that program, you know, I started back in the Bible. Then, I talk with a couple more inmates and we got them. We got a little Bible study we have at the building. You know, I got three or four to start coming back to this little program that we started on our own. I feel glad about that, good about myself, 'cause I got somebody else start back being a Christian and get back in the Bible.

Another inmate described his recruiting efforts to start a small group and the impact it had in his unit:

> We have prayer and Bible study on our own. And actually, man, you see the Lord movin' through them. Through those Bible studies, because guys that you never thought would have attended are comin' all of the sake of being ashamed. They come, they come and they sit and they listen and they participate and you can see a different walk in their life, from that moment because the world still be dealing with them. That sometime Satan will come and steal and rob them, you know what I mean, but for that moment they be, they be like, they be still, they be wantin' to talk about it and after the service, Bible study, is over with, they still want to talk about it. They still want to understand more about what they just felt and understand more about what they just heard. So they be interested. They be very interested.

Beyond the above benefits of small groups described, some inmates also described how taking on leadership positions helped them to achieve a sense of pride and achievement. Consider this example:

> I would have to say that I been doin' the same because I am second in line for the attendance records on Kairos and I have been to every one of the XX services. As a matter of fact, I consider myself the appointed deacon of that church. Me and this other dude that I told you about that is going to be interviewed next, we call out there early just to set up the sound equipment and everything. I pass out tracts. We got these little cards that they put pray requests on that they take back to their church and the people pray for what those people need pray for

so it is kinda like an offering. So I pass those out when the inmates come so I consider myself a deacon for our part of their service.

Another inmate saw himself as responsible for what appeared to be a "church within a church" that operated in his unit:

> I have being doing more in the zone. I got a body of 42 people on the zone and out of 42 people you might have 18 to 20 people participating in your congregation that makes your church. Out of those 20 people I am included with four guys that I characterize as our deacons, but we preach in the open of the other zones. So everybody hears the word even if they don't want to hear the word. It's not that I'm trying to force anything, but there was some guys that we used to get in a room that we minister and I would minister to the people. . . . I prayed about it and brought it to the deacons, we had a meeting on it what should we do, should we bring it out in the open. Once I got my response from the Lord, I knew that the Lord wanted me to take it out in the open and to preach at least once a week in the other zones.

Thus, the inmates discussed at length how surrounding themselves with other religious inmates—whether in formal and informal religious activities—had important attitudinal and behavioral effects. In most cases the various religious activities coalesced to keep religion at the forefront of their minds. This inmate described with great excitement the social support received from his religious activities, and in doing so provides a nice overview of the purpose, content, and impact of all the religious activities at the prison:

> [When] you're around Bible-believin' men and ya'll just sit around and kick the word of God around. Just talk and tell about the goodness of the Lord and start talkin' about your testimony, it's a feeling of the holy ghost. It fills you back up and you can run that race a little bit longer. 'Til you go back down and fill back up, it's like a gas tank. Gotta just keep filling it back up.

## Sharing Faith with Others

Another mechanism the inmates used to maintain their new faith-based identities and to cope with incarceration involved sharing their faith with other inmates. Although it was not discussed as prominently as group religious practice, it is worthy of discussion as a secondary example of the public practice of faith. When religious adherents discuss faith with others, typically it is referred to in evangelical Christian discourse as "sharing your faith" or simply as "sharing" (Tuttle 1999). The purpose of sharing most commonly is evangelical, in that a religious adherent will encourage a nonreligious person to attend a religious service or to experience a conversion. In other cases, however, sharing may involve a religious person helping others deal with various problems or crises, regardless of their spiritual situation. In both cases, religious inmates rely on their faith to guide interactions with others and to keep religion in the foreground.

From the narratives of 63 inmates, three interesting subthemes emerged within the larger theme of sharing faith with others. The first is how inmates frequently reference the scriptural concept of the "Great Commission" as the primary reason for sharing faith. They do so on the basis of verses from the four New Testament gospels. For example, most of the inmates could quote from the Gospel of Matthew where people are told to "go and make disciples of all nations." One inmate who organized informal religious groups in one unit immediately began talking to inmates about starting a small group when he was rotated to a different unit:

> I started to get a little group of my own together when I first came to my building. I came through the door, and I said: "Well, well, well. I see y'all. Y'all don't do anything? Y'all don't pray? Read the word or nothing?" They said, "Nah, man, we don't do anything." I listen to what the young people had to say, and well, if you can be a light, you be that light, you know. Because maybe that's what God want you at, to be that light. Started off with three people and today it have about twenty-some people.

Another inmate reflected on individuals from local religious congregations coming to the prison to share their faith:

> People come down here, take off they time, you know, you got the pastors and the Bibles, were, were visiting your brothers and visiting your sisters you know and you'd think that these brothers, everyone is your brother, you know. And, uh, you think about what God say, you know, "Feed my sheep." And anytime you're speaking the word of God to another individual that's listening, you putting the depth on, you know. It's the seeds have been planted, you know.

Others focused on sharing faith with fellow inmates who were part of prison gangs, or what the inmates at Parchman called "organizations." One inmate described his efforts to help people in those organizations:

> I done took a lot of other brothers who was in an organization and they done start coming to church and everything because they felt like that

they was being misled. And just like, in the Bible, if you can just reach that one soul, that's a blessing right there. I'm not trying to brag or boast, but like, in the zone where I'm at, you probably have 150 organization members, and out of that 150 organization members, I done pulled ten out to start going to church with me.

Second, as the inmates discussed the issue of sharing faith with others, often they used metaphors related to agricultural work. In particular, many inmates made direct reference to Scriptures concerning feeding and taking care of animals. Frequently they discussed the idea of them being "shepherds" and other inmates being "sheep" that needed to be taken care of. Many of the inmates claimed they had a divine imperative to take care of other religious inmates, as well as those who did not identify with a particular faith. One inmate explained why he spent a great deal of time talking with others about his faith:

You think about what God says, you know, "Feed my sheep." And anytime you're speaking the word of God to another individual that's listening, the seed's been planted.

Another inmate explained his emphasis on sharing faith this way:

If we get close to God, we'll be pure and have a happy life, you know. The word of God says, "The man that works his land will have plenty to eat." So I just encourage a lot of young brothers.

Third, and perhaps the most compelling subtheme to emerge from the narratives is that the inmates viewed sharing faith not only as an obligation outlined in Scriptures, but also as a mutually beneficial interaction with others. The inmates described a seemingly counterintuitive situation in which they decided that when they were most depressed, discouraged, or frustrated with prison life, they made a special effort to encourage others who might be facing the same problems. This encouragement of others, in turn, provided much-needed encouragement for them. One inmate described how when he would get depressed, he would seek out others who might also be depressed and try to share his faith to uplift them:

I try to show that I care about another person that is down even though I may be three feet in the ground. If I see somebody next to me that is deeper than I am, I can at least walk up to him and say, "Hey man don't worry about it, Jesus loves you," and walk off. I have done planted my seed and what He's going to do with it is up to Him. It's up to God.

Religious inmates seemed aware that, as Maruna (2001, p. 11) stated so eloquently, "even the most shameful of pasts can be 'put to use' as a sort of moral tale to help guide others in the right direction." The seemingly altruistic act of helping others clearly had reciprocal effects for the ones providing the help. One inmate who identified himself as a lay minister in the Spiritual Life Center explained the cycle of sharing and encouragement:

> Services really just enhanced me and gave me encouragement to be willing to step forward and speak louder. That is just an encouragement for me to be willing to help someone else and tell them that there is a way out and a better [way of] living. Even though you can't get out of the present situation, you can have peace.

Thus, inmates identified sharing their faith as a key part of living a life of faith and attempting to cope with incarceration. The process of sharing faith provided encouragement both to those giving and receiving encouragement. As the inmates shared their faith with others, it enhanced their own religious identities and was a coping resource for the many negative emotions that they experienced. It was clear also that the inmates took great pride in acknowledging that they had encouraged others to attend a religious service or to be converted.

## Summary

In this chapter I presented several emergent themes from my in-depth interviews with 63 inmates in one of the nation's largest prisons. These inmates were all actively involved in faith-based programs at the facility. To use the terminology of Giordano (2002), religious faith appeared to be the primary "hook for change" needed to desist from serious crime and drug use and to move forward in a positive direction. I found that a religious conversion was considered the essential starting point for creating a meaningful commitment to faith and to prosocial behavior for men in prison. The inmates I interviewed articulated key ways in which they created and sustained new faith-based identities.

My findings are in concert with Maruna, Wilson, and Curran (2006, p. 175), who found in their interviews with religious prisoners that "religious conversion can help relieve a sense of psychological crisis because it can provide meaning in the face of meaningless and identify integration when confronted with circumstances that cause individuals to question their sense of identity." Moreover, religious conversions also typically create a shift in how inmates reconcile their past "criminal" selves with their current "straight" selves. Religious conversions provide a new lens through which they can view their lives, and allow them to reinterpret their incarceration as more positive and manageable (Maruna, Wilson, and Curran 2006; Ward and Marshall 2007).

The inmates also discussed the interplay between the private and public practice of faith. Although they described some enjoyment and inspiration derived from their private times of prayer and Scripture study, the inmates spent most of their time describing the enjoyment and necessity of group-oriented religious activities such as formal and informal meetings and sharing their faith with others. Thus, despite the individualistic nature of religious conversion and the new focus on self-improvement, the manner in which inmates accomplished the task of "staying on track" and coping with prison life was primarily social.

Perhaps this comes as a surprise to readers that the social or public aspects of religion were described by the inmates as equally important, if not more important, than the individual or private aspects. From the narratives it was clear that the social support mechanisms of faith were of critical importance in allowing inmates to remain focused and inspired to face the many difficulties and strains of prison life. The true value of faith for prison coping was in the support and accountability structures it created. Even in Maruna, Wilson, and Curran's study of religious prisoners, in which the focus was almost entirely on identity creation and maintenance, the authors acknowledge that "the social identity of the born-again Christian also provides one with membership into a well-established community outside of the prison that welcomes the new convert into the larger fold" (2006, p. 175).

Finally, I think there are some important policy implications for prison administrators and staff based on results from this chapter. Beyond simply making religious programs available to interested inmates, the results suggest some specific strategies for the provision of religious programs. For example, prison chaplains may consider focusing their efforts on creating strong social support networks for religious inmates. Rather than focusing solely on conversion experiences, perhaps chaplains would be better served by helping to foster formal and informal religious practices. They may also work more to connect inmates with local religious parishioners who could provide support for inmates while in prison and after they are released. As found in the narratives of the inmates, the focus on religious conversion is understandable, but the social support mechanisms of faith are what help inmates create a positive self-image and deal with the "pains of imprisonment" (Johnson and Toch 1982). If prison chaplains truly could create a "community of believers," rather than an atomized collection of private adherents, they may observe more positive adjustments to the prison context.

# 6

# Maintaining Change for Women

In the previous chapter I explored how men in prison use faith to cope with incarceration. In this chapter I explore the same topic among women inmates. A separate analysis of prison coping by gender is essential. First, the prison context for women may be unique. Women's prisons differ from those housing men in many quantitative and qualitative ways, including the number and type of programs and treatments offered. Second, the social settings and opportunities may be distinctive. From the location and configuration of cells and units, to the access and seating for the various programs offered, women's prisons often are different in terms of logistics. Third, women prisoners may adapt to their surroundings differently than men. For example, there is evidence to suggest that women inmates are more likely than men inmates to create pseudo-families to help cope with confinement. Fourth, and most importantly for this chapter, women inmates may use religion as a coping mechanism in a different way than men.

To address these empirical issues, I present here an analysis of in-depth interviews with current women inmates who are active in religious programs. As detailed in the Appendix, 40 in-depth interviews were conducted with inmates at the Julia Tutwiler Prison for Women in Wetumpka, Alabama. This maximum-security facility currently houses about 1,200 inmates, and includes the state's only death row for women. The interviewees were involved in a wide range of religious programs, services, and groups. The overwhelming majority of those religious activities could be characterized as evangelical, Christian, or Protestant. I used a similar recruitment strategy and interview guide as I did in the Mississippi men's prison (as described in Chapter 5).

## Background on Women in Prison: Special Challenges

For women inmates, prison life can be more devastating than for men. Interestingly, the study of women in prison is a fairly recent development. For only the past two decades have researchers devoted specific attention to women's prisons and to the experience of prison life among women inmates. One of the most commonly researched topics has been how the incarceration of mothers impacts the development and behavior of their children. The problem is exacerbated in that most states have only one primary prison for women, and usually it is located in a rural area. This makes visitation difficult for the families and friends of inmates, which diminishes their social ties even more significantly.

According to a comprehensive review by Craig (2009), programs for incarcerated women and their children are limited in comparison to those used in the nineteenth and early twentieth centuries. In the 1800s in England, Newgate Prison instituted a program where mothers and children could stay together. Given that the prison also housed male inmates, women keeping their children may have been the only benefit they had. A change came in 1817 when the Association for the Improvement of the Female Prisoners in Newgate was formed, mostly due to the influence of Elizabeth Gurney Fry. The group succeeded in giving women and their children food and clothes, and also created faith-based and life skills classes.

It was not until the mid-nineteenth century in the United States that a large increase in the incarceration of women occurred. In the state of Massachusetts in 1856, the first reformatory was built to house women who committed crimes such as adultery and public drunkenness. Women who were mothers were generally allowed to keep their children with them until age two. For the next century, women's reformatories were quite popular across the United States. The Bedford Hills Correctional Facility in New York, formed in 1901, was one of the most well-known places where women could keep their children for up to one year. However, during the 1930s and 1940s numerous reformatories, many with nurseries, were closed due to economic struggles associated with the Great Depression and World War II. By the 1960s, a federal law prohibited children from being with their mothers in prison. This was due to a prevailing "get tough" attitude that having children in close contact with their deviant mothers was not in the children's best interest (Craig 2009).

Since the 1960s the number of incarcerated women has increased dramatically. A large percentage of those cases is for drug-related offenses, and in those cases typically the children are placed in foster care unless the women have a relative to whom custody can be assigned. Often there is significant emotional and mental trauma associated with separating a mother and her child. Repercussions of this separation can include poor grades, emotional stress, and disruptive behavior for the children, as well as worry, guilt, and anger for the mothers. Therefore, it is imperative for mother and child to at least try to stay in contact while the mother serves her time in prison.

## The Pen Is the Problem

The devastation of prison life for women in Tutwiler Prison was evident throughout their narratives. In fact, this was one of the major differences by gender. Whereas the men inmates tended to focus on problem solving in their new correctional environments (see Chapter 5), the women inmates took the time to delineate and to reflect upon the challenges of incarceration. Thus, before the women inmates described their faith and how it helped them to cope with prison life, they first expanded, often without provocation, on what they were forced to cope with.

Many of the women focused their reflections on the various negative emotions they dealt with during confinement, which seemed to be exacerbated by media depictions of prison life. One long-time inmate reflected on when she first arrived at the facility:

> When I first came to Tutwiler, to be honest, for me being young and here, and watching the TV about what go on inside of the prison institution, I felt scared. I felt alone. I felt . . . basically I felt like it wasn't nothing to live for cause I wasn't with my family. I didn't know nobody. I mean, it was just, I stayed crying. It was just so . . . I didn't understand, and I was around so many people, you know. In prison you're going be with murderers and child molesters, people who done stuff to children and all that, and they would do it to you, or whatever. I just felt so scared and all alone. I felt all alone. I felt lost.

In just this short description she captured the strong emotions of fear of isolation, fear of victimization, sadness, and loneliness. One inmate who had been incarcerated for only about one year described the range of emotions and fears experienced when she first came to prison:

> Oh, I cried a lot. Cause like I said, I was mad. Well, I wasn't mad, I was [wondering] "Why am I here?" When, you know, I'm the one who went through all this, all these years, you know, why me? . . . I was also scared, and I didn't know what to expect. 'Cause like I said, all

you ever heard what people saying and in the movies you know, and things like that. Oh, like never ever take anything for granted out there.

Note how for this inmate the general fear of the unknown quickly gave way to some very specific concerns about the lack of privacy and how this took away the possibility of maintaining a sense of dignity. Another inmate who had been in prison for over five years described her initial fears, as well as the long-term emotional struggles of being incarcerated with other women:

> The first thing I felt coming through that back gate was fear. I was scared, scared. Because it's just fear of the unknown. We've watched all these prison movies, so I didn't know what to expect. I guess, just the majority of the population here, it's like an emotional roller coaster ride. You know, it's hard for women to live together anyway. Put 900 or 1,500 of us together, and it's always something. So you are constantly emotionally imbalanced. You might be happy one minute and ready to tear something apart the next. But my first one was fear, the first time I ever came.

It is interesting how this inmate, in addition to describing her fears, described the special challenges of being surrounded by a large number of other women in the facility and how this caused her to be "emotionally imbalanced." This is an important issue that will be addressed later in this chapter in the section titled "Private Practice."

Other inmates focused on more of the logistical challenges of prison life. This inmate was particularly stressed by her new schedule:

> You have to have a job. You have to do this. You have to get up out your bed at 3:00 in the morning. You have to get up at 3:00 and 4:00 to get breakfast. It was just hard getting used to doing what you weren't used to doing.

Note her trepidation about the difficult work and eating schedules of prison and how those affected something as basic as her sleep-wake cycle. Another inmate elaborated on the challenges of the prison routine:

> The hardest thing to get used to was, for me, [was] the way they run things. They seem to sweat on the small things, [the] things that we take for granted. Like, say for instance, on the weekends, you want to sleep in, but see, you have to be in compliance by a certain time. My Dad put it like this: "Look at it like you're in the military. They either going to try to resign you up in four years, or they're going to let you go." And it's like the military. They tell you how to do everything. It's

lights out, you need to be asleep. It's lights on, you need to get up, you need to get dressed up. Oh it's time to go eat, oh, it's this, that, and the other. And the hardest thing is, it's like, the diet over there, is really not good. And you know what you need [because] everybody is individual with their diets. But I miss those times that I can just go in the refrigerator, and look, see what's on the shelf and close it back. Shopping for my own stuff. Stuff like that. It's a lot of little things that you miss from home.

Another inmate lamented the loss of basic appliances, but in particular lamented the loss of privacy:

Do not take a washing machine for granted. Don't take nothing like that [for granted]. A closed door, don't take it for granted. Cause dignity is something, you know. I'm a very shy person anyway, and it was very hard for me to adjust to showering with seven or eight other women, or excuse me, but sitting down and using the restroom and there's, you know, other ladies there.

Thus, having established from the narratives the major issues that women inmates struggle to cope with, the next step is to understand *how* they cope.

### Studies of Prison Coping for Women

Historically women inmates have received little attention from criminologists, penologists, and policymakers. As the number of incarcerated women rises, however, so too has researchers' interest in measuring how women cope with the prison environment (Warren et al. 2004). According to the bulk of research, women cope in different ways than men. The research indicates that a combination of individual and institutional factors impact the ability of inmates to cope with incarceration. At the individual level, age, educational attainment, criminal history, sentence length, and psychopathology are all strong predictors of prison adjustment and coping (MacKenzie 1987; Warren et al. 2004). Institutional variables linked to prison coping include inmate control of the prison environment, time served, crowding, and limited resources (MacKenzie, Goodstein, and Blouin 1987; MacKenzie, Robinson, and Campbell 1989; Severance 2004).

MacKenzie (1987) was one of the first to study how women cope with prison. To do so she took a random sample of inmates from four prisons in the states of Connecticut, Minnesota, and Illinois. The final sample included 755 women. She grouped the inmates into eight groups according to age and examined differences based on factors such as time served, prior convictions, crime severity, and anxiety. Overall, the age groups were similar in their experiences with the criminal justice system, but in prison there was no direct connection between age and prison coping. Instead, she found that anxiety was the key factor. With increased anxiety came more conflicts with prison personnel and this suggested a struggle to cope with incarceration.

MacKenzie, Robinson, and Campbell (1989) examined how three groups of women inmates adjusted to prison life. The authors split the inmates into three separate categories: inmates who served a short term in prison and who expected to serve a short term, inmates who have served a short term in prison but expect to serve a long term, and inmates who have served a long term in prison and expected to serve a long term. The authors found significant differences in adjustment across the three groups and the primary factor was women's time. Those women who were new to the prison system were more concerned with safety issues than situational ones and were much more likely to join "play families" to help them adjust to prison life. This study is important because it suggests that age and other demographic characteristics of women inmates are less important factors in predicting how they will cope with prison life than their length of sentence and their perceptions of the time they must serve. The authors also found that women inmates were less interested in getting emotional help to cope with the harshness of prison life, but instead needed help to cope with the loss of their material possessions.

As one of the only scholarly book-length works on women in prison, Owen's (1998) *In the Mix* provides a comprehensive analysis of the struggles of women inmates, as well as strategies for coping. Owen conducted an ethnography and in-depth interviews with 300 inmates over the span of three years in one of the nation's largest prisons in California. She describes "in the mix" as a conglomeration of all the positive and negative aspects of prison life. Simultaneously women inmates must "fit in" and "be separate" to survive. Owen found that most women enter prison with the philosophy that they will simply do their time and get back to free society, yet some will "get caught up in the mix of risky and self-defeating behavior" (Owen 1998, p. 8). Similar to the results from MacKenzie's previous studies, Owen found that intimate social relationships were essential in helping women to cope with confinement. In particular, she described in vivid detail the creation and significance of the play family. This relationship provided satisfying emotional bonds with others and even provided a modicum of protection from the self-destructive behavior associated with the mix. Owen (1998,

p. 9) concluded that "surviving the mix is grounded in a woman's ability to develop a satisfying and productive routine within the prison and the nature of her relationships with other prisoners."

Dodge and Pogrebin (2001) also addressed problems facing incarcerated women. In their semi-structured interviews with 54 inmates at a women's correctional facility in the western United States, the authors talked to women about the "collateral costs" of incarceration. The authors found that many of the women suffered from both internal and external shame, especially in regards to their children. Many of the women expressed internal shame for not being able to provide for their children. For an incarcerated woman to gain custody or even visitation opportunities, she must first prove to social services agencies that she is stable enough to take care of her child. This can be achieved by maintaining a job or attending alcohol or drug rehabilitation classes. The problem is that many companies do not want to hire women with criminal records; therefore, these women are not able to provide for their children. One thing that all of the women in the study stressed was the need for emotional support from their families. It provided them with the motivation they needed to continue to make positive changes in their lives, and helped them to know they were not alone.

Snyder, Carlo, and Mullins's (2002) qualitative interviews were focused on the effectiveness of the Mother-Child Visitation Program (MCVP) that operated in a women's prison in the midwestern United States. The program included visitation opportunities and parenting classes. There were 58 mothers interviewed, of which 31 were in the program and 27 were on the waiting list. The author found that MCVP fostered improved relationships between mother and child when the mother was enrolled in the program. Even in comparison to women who were waiting for the program and were getting their own visits on prison visitation days, women in MCVP reported a much stronger connection with their children.

Severance (2005) focused more on how social networks could impact coping for women inmates. She conducted 40 in-depth interviews in an Ohio prison to explore how they perceive their relationships with other inmates and how it affected their ability to adapt to the prison environment. Severance found that social support was critical for women's ability to adapt to the struggles of prison life. Pseudo-families, friendships, and lesbian relationships were the three main types of social relationships she found, and women with those social ties were more likely to adapt fully and quickly. She found also that the element of trust, which outsiders typically believe is nonexistent in prison, was highlighted in the women's narratives. To find at least one person in which to confide was an enormous help to the women.

A quantitative study by Sandifer (2008) highlights another major obstacle for a growing number of women who are incarcerated while their children are young, which is the lack of parenting skills. During their imprisonment, they are unable to develop parenting skills that would otherwise be obtained by living with their children in a normal setting. After the trauma of separation, a returning parent gives the child an opportunity to cope better with anxiety, depression, and stress. The program studied by Sandifer was not only a visitation program for mothers and children, but also had a standardized class meeting. The parenting class met three hours per day, twice per week for a 12-week period with goals including: parenting knowledge on discipline, education, communication, and providing emotional support for their children. A pre- and post-test evaluation was administered and the results showed a "significantly positive change likely resulting from the parenting program in inmate mothers' parenting knowledge" (Sandifer 2008, p. 423).

## Faith and Coping in Tutwiler Prison

Thomas and Zaitzow (2006) argue that the use of religious programs in prison is a unique opportunity to channel inmates' energies to something meaningful and beneficial. Even though religion has been a part of the US correctional system since its inception, there is some controversy because uninhibited religious expression may create concerns relating to security and safety. However, religious programs provide an opportunity for inmates to change their behavior. The authors summarized the impact of religion on inmates before and after incarceration and offered 10 reasons why religious programs should be expanded in prisons. Some of these reasons include: religion contributes to the feeling of well-being, it reduces stress, and improves their overall mental and physical health (Thomas and Zaitzow 2006).

Giordano's (2002) study of crime desistance among adult women offenders is an important heuristic for understanding the narratives of the women I interviewed at Tutwiler prison. Giordano described a process of "cognitive transformation," whereby offenders craft a new or "replacement" self that helps them to move beyond their prior criminal identity and lifestyle. This identity work is thought to help them transition away from crime and drugs and to direct their focus toward more prosocial lines of behavior in the future.

Accompanying this identity transformation are various external "hooks for change," such as children, romantic partners, prison treatment, and religion. Summarizing the value of these external motivations for change, the authors argue that "successful hooks for change offered more in the way of a blueprint for behavior and facilitated the development of an alternative view of self that was seen as fundamentally incompatible with criminal behavior" (Giordano 2002, p. 1038). This was one of the first comprehensive studies of crime desistance for women, and my research can be seen as a next step in the development of this literature. In the remainder of this chapter I will expand their work by providing a more comprehensive view of how religion may serve as one of the hooks for change in the desistance process among women offenders.

As I move now to the narratives of the Tutwiler women about how they use religious faith to cope, let me note first what I considered a fascinating observation. The women described how faith was more than just a coping resource or an additional help. For the large majority of them, faith was the only thing in prison they considered critical. The oldest inmate in our sample, who was serving a life sentence, summarized the role that faith played in her emotional, social, and physical survival:

> The belief in the Lord has to play a major part. Because if you don't believe in Him, then you're going to be that crazy person on all this medication, being zoned out and can't even talk because of the way you have nothing else. So I think choosing faith and the belief in God is just the only way. There's no modern medication [that can do the same]. If I was on death row, there is no amount of medication in this world that would wanna keep me from killing myself. There's no way I could sit in death row for two years or [even] a week if I knew my only destination, my only punishment, was to be killed. I'd rather have it done or completely turn every ounce of my being to the Lord to be able to live through that. So faith is the only way: the only way to survive in here.

For this inmate and for nearly all of the women I interviewed, faith was not an occasional program or ritual, but a way of life.

## Public Practice of Faith

Clear and colleagues (2000) were some of the first scholars to discuss the group phenomenon of faith in prison. They noted how for some inmates the religious experience has less to do with individual experiences and more to do with faith groups formed while in prison. Shifts in the prison environment can occur as inmates come and go, but when inmates share their feelings about religion, attend services and study groups, and have day-to-day interactions with other religious inmates, the group aspects of faith may help inmates to cope.

### Group Services

Women inmates at Tutwiler frequently described many of the group religious activities in which they were involved. These included services conducted two or three times per week in the chapel, group scripture studies, and a choir group. One inmate described how she benefited from the group services, as well as how she could tell the difference between others involved and those who were not:

> Because we can all look around and see who is doing their time versus time doing them. And you can see somebody that's older and how they carry themselves. And you will know that they're in their Bible and … choose what programs to do. You know, garbage in, garbage out. You know that there's a peace about them, that there's a serenity about them. And when they are aware of a situation in our lives, there's a little hand on your shoulder saying, "Honey, I'm praying for you." Those things, it's the only way to do time. And you also know the ones that are absolute hell raisers, ripping and roaring. They're always going to be in segregation, they're always going to be running up and down the halls.

The claim from this quote appears to be that without involvement in faith-based social groups, the women will be in a position where their "time is doing them." Another inmate summarized the impact of the services and all of the relationships created from them. In doing so she tried to imagine what the prison would be like if faith-based programs were eliminated:

> I'm trying to envision a day without [religious services] and I can't. Plain and simple. Even if I'm having a horrible day, I know there are good friends, there are people involved in the services on the outside that are praying. I know that even a neighbor, somebody that's sleeping beside me is praying. Women that have left a program, an end of sentence, or a parole. I know they and their family members, if it's not specifically for those that are in prison, for those that are feeling helpless in prison, I know there is somebody praying.

Throughout the narratives the inmates claimed that attendance in the religious services provided a wide range of spiritual and emotional benefits. For this inmate involvement in various religious groups, and the social support received from them, helped to break an addiction she had been struggling with for many years:

> I've been here almost a year come April. And like I said, when I first got here, when I just made up my mind, I knew that God gave me this body. This is His vessel. It doesn't even belong to me so I just kind of made up my mind I didn't want to smoke. So now I just strive . . . and attend everything that comes through the door that's [a] chapel service. I go because everything is for me. Well, I take that back. I don't go to the Islamic and Catholic mass, but everything else I try to go. Cause I know everything is not going to be for me, but something that everybody says that come there, something in the message that's for me.

Many inmates described the strong emotional highs associated with attendance at the group services. It was not unusual for prison staff and members of local congregations to attend some of the services along with the inmates, and this created a unique environment. One inmate described the high she experienced at a service where the prison warden was present:

> I've gone to some [services] where it's just nothing but prayer. And you can actually feel the difference spiritually when all you hear is just everybody. And it's moving because you actually hear the Warden quietly weeping or crying, so you know that there's something in what was said that moved him. I've done it myself. A word or two, and then all of a sudden you feel like spiritually, there's been a breakthrough.

The inmate said that this spiritual experience was not available if she were alone. Instead, it was the interactions with religious others and watching the reactions of others that caused her to "feel the spirit" as well. Sociologists might describe this in terms of a contagion effect, wherein the actions and emotions of some group members produce a concordant response from others in the group. Clearly this was the draw for the women at Tutwiler who were most involved in religious services and small groups. They appeared to have a confident anticipation that "God is going to do something" in all of their group activities.

Finally, I observed from the narratives that for most of the women the culmination of their involvement in religious services and groups was that they took on a faith-based reputation. Depending on the situation, that reputation could be positive or negative. Although it could create a sense of shared experience and camaraderie among like-minded others, in Tutwiler, having a reputation as religious could cause some women to be the targets for ridicule, arguments, and even physical altercations. For nearly all of the women I interviewed, however, they claimed that their faith-based reputation was a positive thing. Take for example this summary where an inmate described how her faith and attendance at the religious services became like a master status:

> I love that Christian identity. You know, people here surely wouldn't know me from anything else. If they know me, that's [religious services] what they're know me from. . . . So if they know me, that's how they know me. Either from going to church or they know me as being a Christian.

### Sharing Faith with Others

The next example of public practice is sharing faith with others. I asked the women inmates if they shared faith with others, if they tried to influence others to attend religious programs, and if they had scripture study and prayer groups in their units. Some of the inmates said they did not try to talk to others about religion because there was a chance that it could cause confrontations. Others said they tried to share their faith with other inmates to help them become better people. This inmate describes how God sends her "problem people" that she can help:

> God always lead me to people who have problems or in a situation. And I'll say: "Now you see that? You just got through arguing. Now what you need to do is come on, let's go to church tonight and let's hear some good. Get your spirit right. Let's get your soul right. C'mon go with me." Or I say: "Look, if God come back right now, I don't have time to tell you to c'mon. I got to go. You know what I'm saying? And we're close to the end. There's so much going on." . . . Before I know it, they be: "Okay, I going to church tonight. You see I'm ready." And that's how they'll go. And when they get there, they really enjoy it, because it be something for them to hear. God just be speaking to them. It be so interesting. God be speaking to them.

Embedded within the narratives of sharing faith is the idea that the women see inviting others to religious services or groups as a spiritual obligation or expectation. Many of the women were adamant that all believers in the prison setting should be inviting others. In the following quote, one inmate recounts a series of questions she typically asks other inmates to assess their interest in religion and to determine how she can get them to attend services:

I think everyone should be inviting people to services. [I] ask them: "Do you want hear the Word of the Lord? Do you feel a need for the Lord. Are you hurting inside? Do you understand that coming to the chapel you will have a chance to worship? You will have a chance to hear whether it be preaching or scripture class. Are you a serious studier of the Word? There's no pressure to convert or anything, but if you just want to hear the Word you're more than welcome [to attend]."

Another inmate described a very similar approach to sharing her faith:

The first thing I would ask them is "do you sing?" You know. And sometimes they do, sometimes they do. Well, you know we have a choir. And if you like to be interested, 'cause we sing religious songs, we just sing musical songs, we don't sing just all religious songs. And if they didn't do that then I'd say: "I want you come to church with me. Go to church with me tonight." I'd always invite them to church with me. Sometimes they'd go and enjoy it and come back and sometimes they wouldn't. But you know, you can't make them, you can't make them keep coming back. You can only encourage them to go.

For other religious inmates the focus on sharing faith was less on inviting others to attend religious services, and more on trying to help others work through difficult situations and being willing to listen to their concerns. Once that trust and concern was established, she tried to discuss her faith with them and encourage them to embrace faith as well:

If I see someone down, I don't know how to explain it, I'll tell people that I'll listen. Sometimes when you try to bring up God or something, then people are just kinda like: "Go away. Or I gotta go do something." Usually it's the people that are willing to listen that I'll talk to them about God and about, you know, what Jesus Christ did for you. Or not really what he did for you, but how much He loves you and stuff. It's the people that want to listen, you know, that I talk to.

It was clear that the women subscribed to the well-circulated evangelical mantra that "people will not care how much you know, until they know how much you care."

*Dealing with Conflict*

The final example of public practice is how the religious inmates claimed that they used their faith when dealing with conflict. The inmates described how they kept from arguing with others and how they dealt with threats and confrontations. Most readers can relate to the difficulties of dealing with people in everyday life, and so imagine that those difficulties are increased exponentially in the prison context.

Many of the inmates referred to the concept of "bridling the tongue" from the Epistle of James as their primary method for conflict avoidance. This is the scripture to which the women referred: "If anyone thinks he is religious and does not bridle his tongue but deceives his heart, this person's religion is worthless." One inmate explained the concept this way:

> I have to pray and ask God to bridle my tongue. I'm quicker today to walk away. When I first started coming to this prison, I couldn't do that. I fought a lot. So today, and it's back to my acceptance [of God], I've got to allow people to be who they are, but a lot of times I have to pray, because my temper started steaming up. I'd be like, "Lord, hold my tongue. Give me the strength." And I just walk or I go get a book or I turn on the radio and listen to Hallelujah FM. But this time in prison, that's what have helped me.

Another inmate described the same concept in this manner:

> Oh, you have to bite your tongue. You bite your tongue a lot, and you go: "Ok. What would the Lord do, what would God do right now? What would the Lord do right now?" But sometimes you don't have time to react like that. Sometimes your flesh speaks out before your religious part does, you know. Like I said, you have to stay focused, and it's hard to stay focused in here cause, you have to practice. You have to practice staying focused on certain things. Because it's not just something you're going to do, it's a learning process.

Another woman described the idea of bridling the tongue not so much as a personal response to conflict derived from scriptural principles, but as a supernatural response over which she had little control:

> To be honest with you, I have had so many people come up and say stupid things to me, but God has put a muzzle over my mouth. I'm serious. I am not able to use no profanity. In fact I can just say, "She said that to me, and I didn't even say nothing back." It's just amazing how God just cuts it out, He don't let me say nothing bad to nobody no more. I used to be the worst person. I would talk about you, your children, don't even know anything about them. Just down you, because I didn't want you to get to me, hurt me, so I always hurt you first. But now, you could say anything, and I really don't say nothing real bad.

As they described their strategies for avoiding conflict with other inmates, the women seemed cognizant of the negative repercussions of those conflicts. One woman discussed how she had to "just walk away" from negative people because they were "like kerosene to a flame." By staying away from negative people, she claimed that the flames of conflict could not burn:

> I would say the most important [thing] that I have to do in dealing with conflict is not be hypocritical. Because if I portray that my spirituality, my religiousness is something that is only a convenience for me, I'm not being real. . . . I need to spend more time being nourished by prayer by, by reading Scripture, by being around somebody that is going to be a calming influence rather than pouring kerosene while I'm thinking. Flicking a Bic lighter. All that is available to me. It's my choice what I want.

Another inmate described the importance of walking away from conflict, but struggled to articulate whether her response to conflict was self-driven or God-driven. Either way, she claimed to be resolute in trying to avoid negative situations:

> I just walk away. And so, Jesus in me is who handles my problems now. I allow Him, I've learned how to be submissive to Him in my life, in my flesh. There have been times when somebody has said something smart, or I woke up in a bad mood and somebody just look at me all lopsided and you want to say something to them, but I rebuke Satan. In my mind, I'm like, "I'm not going to fall for that. I'm not going for it this time." . . . You know, that's why it's so important for us to have these services and to be taught. Because if don't nobody teach you how to handle a situation or how to handle something in your life, you're not going to handle any differently than the way you always have. And that's what God has done for me. He's taught me how to handle it now, or how to let Him handle it.

## Private Practice of Faith

Even as the women inmates described how the public practice of faith could be helpful in coping with incarceration, it was clear that the majority (29 of the 40 interviewees) preferred the private practice of faith. This is the exact opposite of what I observed in the narratives from the religious inmates in the men's prison (see Chapter 5). For the women at Tutwiler, private prayer, scripture study, and keeping to themselves were the three elements of private practice. In doing so, the women claimed that they could foster a "spiritual mindset" that would help them to stave off the deleterious effects of prison life. Here I note a connection with Clear and colleagues' (2000) description of the individual benefits of religious experience. For some religious adherents, the individual experience of faith is considered the most powerful and most "real" of all experiences. Moreover, in evangelical Protestant denominations, a personal relationship with a higher power and consistent personal "quiet time" are requirements for being a person of faith.

### Staying Prayed Up

Many of the women described prayer as the first and most important element of their private practice of faith. Although evangelical Protestants vary in terms of how and when they use this religious ritual, for the women interviewed at Tutwiler prayer was described as a nearly constant behavior. One inmate discussed how she used prayer each day:

> I pray. I pray all day. I go in the bathroom in school over at the college and I pray. I pray because there's so much that really aggravate you in this place depending on your mindset. You know, sometimes I'm thinking about my kids and I'm missing them, and someone can really get on your nerves that talks a lot. And then I go in the bathroom and I pray. Or I may be talking to you and I'm praying. So my prayer life has really increased since I got in this prison.

Interesting to note from this quote above is that she uses prayer primarily as a means of survival and to cope with all of the potential aggravations of prison life. Another inmate reflected on how often she prayed and how it provided a shield against negative individuals and situations:

> It helps a lot, because before I got here, I always thought that when you pray to God, pray in the morning when you wake, and you pray at night when you go to bed. But now I find that in my daily walk, I pray all day. I find myself sitting in class and praying. It's like it builds your spirit up, and your spirit takes control. Whereas, you're not even thinking about praying, and you're doing something else, but there's so much stuff going around, and going on around you. I find myself sitting around and the prayer's going on in my spirit without me, you know, voicing words. So now I find that I just pray, I do a lot of praying. Just sometimes walking down the hall, just sitting on my bed.

Whereas many in the general public might articulate other motivations for prayer—such as closeness to a higher power, intercession for others, and forgiveness for wrongdoing—in prison it may be that prayer becomes more self-oriented and related to coping with the many struggles inherent in prison life. This inmate described similar spiritual struggles and her use of prayer to overcome them:

> A lot of the time I walk down the hallway, and I don't be trying to ignore nobody, but I be talking to the Lord cause I can feel the presence of evilness as I pass these dorms. And I be like, "Jesus, Jesus. Hallelujah Lord." I be trying to keep my spirit straight. Because Satan's over here, he's going to jump in me. You know what I'm saying? So I have to stay focused. When I leave out that dorm, I'm always saying, "Jesus, Jesus.' I sing a song. If I don't complete the whole song, I just sing something to get my spirit right. Because it's a lot you have to tackle out there. So I have to stay prayed up all the time.

It was clear that her only hope of survival and of "staying straight" was that she spend a great deal of time in prayer every day. Another inmate who had worked for several years in the prison's kitchen described how prayer was the only thing that she thought could help her to survive a typical workday. When asked how often she prayed, she said:

> Every day. Every morning. When I'm at work and [other inmates] makes me mad, I have to pray to keep from cussing. Cussing them out, because everybody's going to feel they're right or wrong in their way. So, yeah, I pray a lot. And prayer's the only thing that'll get you through this. And anything else is uncivilized, because it's the works of the devil.

Another inmate explained how an active prayer life helped her to stay focused on her faith and allowed her to be insulated from others:

> See when I turn my life onto the Lord, I no longer do the things that I used to do. I don't; [instead], I pray for people. Like when I walk the hallway and I see them cursing and disrespecting somebody, I just immediately start praying. I don't go to them and say, "Look, you better not." I can't do that, cause I did it. Nobody could tell me anything. So what I do, I pray for that individual. You know what I'm saying? And I know God will answer prayer, and He do changes things, so I continue to go on. But I know with prayer, being that I'm a warrior for the Lord, a prayer warrior.

*Staying in the Word*

In addition to private prayer done on a consistent basis, the women also described the value of scripture reading. One inmate incarcerated for a violent crime described her typical day:

> I've learned in my Christian walk how to be humble. And humility is something that goes along with being grateful for His spirit with me. I ask Him every day to let me be humble. Every day when I wake, I give Him my mind, heart, body and soul to do with as He pleases. And I give myself to Him every day. I try to start my day off with the Word, with reading the Word and meditating on Him. And if you get yourself focused, if you let Him be a daily part of your life, every minute of it [is] better.

This inmate believed that reading scriptures on a daily basis helped her to become humble, grateful, and focused. She even specified a certain time of day when she thought the reading could help her most. Others described similar benefits of reading, but only if they did it on a consistent basis. This inmate described how she always tried to shut out everyone—which is no simple task in the prison setting—and spend time alone reading scriptures each day:

> I feel better when I'm reading my Bible. I can get on my bed and read my Bible and sit there and act like nobody else is around, because I really feel like that's the way I need to be.

Another inmate described how she recently attempted to increase her religious commitment and the role that reading scriptures played in that:

> And it was just a feeling that overcome me by talking, and it's been with me ever since. It's just been different for me. And it was not like that any other time. I did that a lot of times, but this time it was different. When I did it, I felt it. And this time, I understand my Bible more. It's like I catch myself reading my Bible more. It's like He knows I want to change. And He knows when I'm being real and when I'm not being real.

It appears that a cycle of faith is being described here, and it was a common theme in 29 of the 40 narratives. The women wanted to change to a more positive mindset and to more positive behaviors, and saw a relationship with a higher power as the root of this change. To accomplish change, they read scriptures more often. They claimed that this reading brought them closer to the higher power as they internalized various scriptural precepts such as "being holy" and "loving others." As they internalized those precepts, they became even more motivated to change to a more pro-social self and to read scriptures more often. The cycle continued from there. Consequently, as the women saturated themselves in private reading and meditating on scriptures, they claimed that religion became part of their identity. In particular it became the way that others defined them:

> Sometimes I have felt like people talking about me reading my Bible so much. . . . They see me reading my Bible, and that also I'm always kind and trying to handle things right. And that will define who I am in God. And people come and ask me questions. They'll ask me if they need to know something about the Bible. They'll ask me!

### Staying to Myself

The final example of the private practice of faith to emerge was that religious inmates tended to isolate themselves from others, especially from those they considered to be "trouble." For many this behavior was linked to the scriptural concept of "separation," while for others it was a more pragmatic decision to avoid interruptions to their private times of prayer and scripture study. One long-time inmate explained why she kept to herself:

> We [religious inmates] don't fit in with everyone else. We don't want to talk about so-and-so, and we don't want to watch you and your girlfriend kiss, and we don't want to cuss somebody out. We don't want to do those things anymore. And it's not us, it's God in us. But it's things that, as Christians, I believe we have to separate ourselves from in our daily walk in order to keep our spirit right. Like I said [it is] about feeding your spirit.

Another inmate explained her reclusiveness this way:

> The other big adjustment that I've had to make here is I've had to stay mainly to myself and to God. I have to take every worry, every thought, everything to God. My thing is staying, not getting close to people in here, because if I get close to people in here, they can hurt me, you know. So my thing is staying to myself. And also another thing is for me, when I see other things going on, I have to not even listen to it. I cannot even be a part of anything that goes on around me.

The obvious next question that I needed to ask the inmates was this: what or whom are you separating yourself from? My conclusion was that the women claimed to have a very strong sense of positive versus negative people and things, but they struggled to articulate any details about the negative. Consider this example:

> You can tell negative people from the positive. Positive person always going around giving folks an encouraging word, and they stay in the church. You know, I just know how to separate myself from people anyway, from the negative and the positive. I just know just how to deal with it. So, you can tell the negative people always doing negative things. Always saying negative stuff. The positive always going to have something positive to say.

The inmate described two characteristics of a "positive person" but could make only the tautological argument that negative people are always "doing negative things" or "saying negative stuff." Likewise, another inmate seemed to know intuitively whom and what to avoid, but provided little in the way of description other than to say that some inmates were "trouble." Note the generic way that she described the people she avoids:

> I don't associate with the people who do get in trouble. I just stay my distance from them. A lot of people know me, they speak to me. But I just speak back, and I don't hold conversations with them. I say "hello" and that's pretty much how you're going to stay out of trouble here. And don't get caught where you're not supposed to be. Don't get caught doing things you're not supposed to do.

One additional approach, albeit least common among the women inmates I interviewed, is that they established a consistent routine and set of standards that should not be disturbed by others. Rather than going out of their way to avoid negative influences, a small percentage of the women claimed to create an insular environment where only the most religious inmates would attempt to interact with them. In an interesting twist, it appeared that these women isolated themselves to the point that "troublemakers" would avoid them instead of the converse. This inmate described the counter-intuitive scenario.

> Believe it or not, when people describe me, they talk about God because they remember who I used to be from the time I was in prison before. And now I'm entirely different. It's like, I don't listen to R&B [rhythm and blues], rock and roll, you know, booty shaking, anything like that. I only do Gospel, because I need to feed my spirit. So I try to

do all things that are going to feed my spirit. And they kind of tiptoe around me a little bit. It's kinda like they identify me as, I don't know what they call me, but you know, they do different things. Whereas, like on radio day, they all say, "Well, you can listen to the radio today." And they'll go downstairs cause they don't really want to listen to it. But because they know that's what I want to listen to [faith-based music and programming], they'll alternate with me and let me have radio on that day.

## Summary

In this chapter we learned that religious inmates in the women's prison claimed that private times of prayer and scripture reading, as well as staying to themselves, were the key predictors of coping effectively with prison life. This finding is unique in comparison with findings from the handful of other studies discussed previously. Additionally, the private coping strategies preferred by the women inmates are different than for the men who, overall, preferred the public practice of faith (see Chapter 5). Beyond the comparison to previous research, my findings here stand in contrast to the common stereotype that women are more social than men and thus prefer social groups. The narratives from Tutwiler inmates suggest that the social nature of women, in fact, *takes away from* a preference for the social aspects of faith. Nearly three quarters of the inmates I interviewed discussed how difficult it was for the roughly 1,000 women to live together. Consequently, for the religious inmates to stay focused on their faith, they claimed that they had to focus on themselves.

I note also that embedded within the private practice of faith is the idea that the women wanted to create a "spiritual mindset" while in prison. Evidently it was not enough for them to engage daily in religious rituals; instead, they claimed that an overarching emotional focus on faith had to be established if they were to survive the prison experience. Asked to explain this idea of a spiritual mindset, one inmate offered what I think is a comprehensive and illuminating summary:

To me it's a mind thing. It's up to you. It's up to you how you want to do your time. If you want to do it sitting around, crying, and being depressed over this situation or whatever, and worry yourself about it, it's up to you if you want to move forward. You just got to read your Bible. And if you believe what the Word say, what God say in his Word, I mean, it's up to you how you want to do your time. You feel me? It's up to you. . . . You have to let go and let God. I had to do that. I had to realize that it was up to me how I wanted to do my time.

Given the paucity of research on women offenders, especially in regard to faith, I think it is important to note the uniqueness of my sample of 40 religious converts from a women's prison. In previous chapters I have often referenced Maruna's (2001) groundbreaking work on the crime desistance process. Although his findings on the common characteristics of successful desisters are not gender specific, he does note the unique context of studying women religious converts:

> The stigma attached to female offenders and drug addicts, especially those with children, is probably greater than that for male offenders. . . . Yet, society also probably holds out greater hope that more female offenders can be reformed. In popular and media accounts, for instance, women offenders are much more often portrayed as victims of circumstances. An example of this was seen in Texas recently, when traditional death penalty supporters fought against the execution of Karla Faye Tucker, Although the alleged rationale for this unexpected compassion was that Tucker was a born-again Christian, surely she was not the first inmate on death row to accept God into his or her life. This example hardly suggests that female ex-offenders have an easier time proving their reform, however. After all, Tucker was executed, despite the efforts of the Christian Right. (Maruna 2001, p. 176)

Finally, as noted throughout this chapter, the themes I found are in concert with the work of Giordano (2002) on crime desistance for women offenders. That author described how ex-offenders experienced a "cognitive transformation," in which they crafted a new or "replacement" self that helped them move beyond their prior criminal identities and lifestyles. This identity work is thought to help them transition away from crime and drugs and to direct their focus toward more prosocial lines of behavior in the future. As part of that identity transformation, the women in Giordano's study described many "hooks for change" that would facilitate the maintenance of a more prosocial identity and set of behaviors. Her's was one of the first comprehensive studies of crime desistance for women, and my research here has expanded the literature by providing a comprehensive view of how religion may serve as one of the "hooks for change" in the desistance process for women offenders.

# 7

# The Halfway House Experience

Having explored in the previous chapter how women use faith to cope with prison, I now explore how women use faith to cope with a different correctional context. In this chapter the focus is on the narratives of 70 residents of a women's transitional facility or "halfway house" in the southern United States (hereafter "the center"). As detailed in the Appendix, the center currently houses nearly 450 women and children. Residents fall into one of three categories: (1) women under supervised release from state prison, (2) women under court-ordered probation, (3) women who are self-admitted for drug addiction or other issues. It is estimated that about 90 percent of residents experienced drug or alcohol addiction at least once prior to arrival.

Each interview began with a discussion of events that led to their admission to the center. For most this meant a lengthy discussion of previous crimes and drug use. Interviewees were then asked about the religious and educational programs at the center and how they were able to adjust. They were asked how, if at all, they had changed since admission to the center and whether the faith-based aspects played a part in that change. The women were then asked to describe difficult situations encountered at the facility and whether religion helped them to cope with those situations. Each interview ended with a discussion of the future for each resident after release and how faith might impact that future. Pseudonyms are used here for the names of residents to protect their identities.

## Claiming Change

The first overarching theme to emerge was that the women claimed to be undergoing dramatic lifestyle changes. Most had tried unsuccessfully to make such changes previously, and some portrayed the power of addiction as stronger than any higher loyalties to others or to themselves. Nevertheless, they claimed that this time they would be successful in overcoming drugs and crime because they had a stronger spiritual base. They described their change process with strong imagery such as "breaking the chains" of drugs and crime. The women combined reasons to be clean with a recognition of God as a catalyst for change. This created a sharp contrast between their prior addicted and criminal selves and their current drug-free selves. In their view God was an all-powerful force, and although drugs and crime were stronger than them, they could defeat those forces when they combined their personal desires with a newfound commitment to faith. The seed of this new self was the belief that they were in the midst of real change, and that successful recovery was possible this time.

For all of the narratives of success in transitional and rehabilitation centers emanating from facilities across the United States, unfortunately, the large majority of narratives end with relapse and hopelessness. In making claims of religious conversion or recommitment, residents at the center seemed cognizant that change would be difficult and that many in the general public would be doubtful of the possibility of dramatic change, especially for those who had served time in prison and had drug and alcohol problems. Skeptics abound of jailhouse conversions and of sudden cases of people "finding religion" during stressful life events such as incarceration. Residents seemed aware that their chances for success in society indeed were a long shot.

Despite the difficult nature of the journey, however, the women seemed intent on reaching their goals of faith, sobriety, and responsibility. Tara explained:

> I already been here before about two years ago but just like I said was coming for the wrong reasons. It really saved my life. I got saved and got baptized. . . . I'm really tryin' to change my life for the better cause the way I was living, it's just not the way to live.

The interviewees seemed to address potential critics directly, but not necessarily in a defensive manner as might be anticipated. Almost as if on a quest to prove skeptics wrong, Felicity noted:

> I was a completely different person when I first came in here. I wanna show that girls here, they can change.

The women held firm in their belief that they could successfully "break the chains" of crime, in particular of drug and alcohol addiction.

As they presented their claims of undergoing real change, routinely it was observed that the impetus for this change was the women experiencing a major life-affirming event (e.g., the birth of child) or a major negative event termed "rock bottom." Indeed, all of the interviewees cited these reasons for wanting to leave the criminal lifestyle. Julianna identified the final push for her to leave her life of drug addiction as the birth of a nephew. Describing her new goal of sobriety she stated:

> I really want it. I was willing to let go of all the guys, the friends, the atmosphere, the street life. . . . I don't want that. I have a nephew to raise.

Although she expressed a desire to get clean before her nephew was born, "stepping up" in place of her sister to care for her nephew was the primary motivation for the change she claimed.

This idea of a life-affirming event serving as an impetus for change and crime desistance is similar to themes found in the work of Giordano (2002). Those authors conducted a long-term study of delinquent youths in Ohio. Later in life, as adult offenders, many of them identified various "hooks for change" that facilitated their desistance from most crimes and deviant behaviors. Prominent among the hooks was the desire to connect or reconnect with children and romantic partners. Giordano (2002) found that the hooks were not only external motivators for change, but helped to create fundamental shifts in identity among the offenders.

While a specific life-affirming event motivated many of the women to desist from crime, for most the motivation was derived from an extreme low point such as broken family relationships, loss of a child or loved one, feelings of hopelessness, or loss of material possessions. The most common low point was being sentenced to prison or court-ordered probation. Most of the women described their low points as "hitting rock bottom." The concept of hitting rock bottom commonly is linked with the founders of Alcoholics Anonymous (AA), who used it to describe the feeling they experienced just prior to making the decision to seek help (Kurtz 1979).

Since the inception of the Alcoholics Anonymous program, hitting bottom has been a crucial step; however, what defines hitting bottom has changed since the program began in the 1930s. Although many recognize rock bottom as an internal feeling of loss and hopelessness, in most cases reported by AA the feeling manifested itself through a loss of material possessions, a job, or loved ones. According to Kurtz (1979), early AA members searched gutters and hospitals for individuals who embodied the despair and degradation they felt. As time went on members began to realize that hitting bottom did not have to mean losing everything. He went on to note that "if somehow the alcoholic could be given an insight into the spiritual unreality of his life by breaking through his denial and bringing him face to face with the absolute nature of his dependence on alcohol—then the alcoholic 'hit bottom'" (Kurtz 1979, p. 211). In more recent times hitting rock bottom has become associated with all individuals struggling with difficult life situations such as drugs, alcohol, crime, and homelessness.

Many of the women at the center described the hitting bottom experience as a type of spontaneous psychological moment, while others described it as a downward spiral that eventually led them to realize that change was needed. Kyrie described in vivid details her experience of hitting rock bottom:

> Walking around the streets of Nashville, doing anything and everything, still just running. It's like, "You did all that because of alcohol?" Well, it's a lot more than alcohol. No I never shot up, no I don't do crack, no I don't do meth, but there are root issues of something there. It could have been food. It could have been anything. I would've just kept filling that void. That was definitely my worst and I would've never thought I'd do that in a billion years. I mean, never. Could you imagine yourself doing that? No. Could you imagine yourself all of a sudden out on the streets of Nashville selling your body just to get a beer and lay your head down? I mean, who does that?

Whether the impetus was a positive or negative life situation, the women claimed that they had a dramatic point in which the change process began. This finding again is consistent with the work of Giordano (2002). She crafted a theory of cognitive transformation to describe the shifts that facilitate the crime desistance process. Although she identified religion as one of the hooks for change, it was not an overcharging theme and thus not well developed. Thus, the results presented here can be seen as an expansion of the hooks that are common among women attempting to desist from drugs and crime.

While the desire to overcome addiction was thought to be vital for recovery, these women thought that simply wanting to change was not enough. This belief was born from their failed attempts at recovery. The women acknowledged that they had tried to go straight many times before, but were unsuccessful. Those who failed to stay clean in the past portrayed the power of addiction as stronger than higher loyalties to others or to their own personal desires. They claimed that dramatic change was taking place in their lives, but only because their personal desires were now coupled with a commitment to God.

In Athens's (1995) classic conceptual work, "Dramatic Self-Change," he describes a five-stage process of change, which ranges from the total dissolution of the old self in the first stage to the social segregation from others who might undermine the newly created self. The stage that seems relevant to my findings here is the "provisional" stage. Athens describes this as the stage when individuals attempt to piece together a new and stronger self to take the place of the old self. What I found is that women at the center were engaged in this process, but did not think that they could create the new self without the help of a higher power.

It was not uncommon for the residents to make statements about the importance of "surrendering to God's will." Although the women described the personal effort and willpower it took to "get clean" and to start their lives again, they did not see it as possible for these efforts to be successful without God directing their lives. Kyrie claimed that her success came from:

> Letting go and letting God, because it's all in His hands. He already has everything planned out for you and all you got to do is walk it out.

Jessa explained the reasons she thought that it was necessary for her to change:

> It just came to me that, you know, God's in control. If it's God's will for me to go to prison that sucks, but there's a reason for it. It's gotta be a reason for it. 'Cause I mean, the reason might be I graduate this program, I get out, shoot up some dope a week later, and die. As opposed to that, what could have happened, I go to prison and that don't happen. You know what I mean? So you gotta believe in something. You gotta believe that there is a reason for all this. Because it don't make sense any other way.

The center's unique programs helped many of the women see this time as a true recovery. Topanga highlighted her desire to get clean this time when asked about her previous relapse, stating:

> I wasn't ready. . . . It's just the choice. Not being able to do what you want to do, not being forced or nothing. I don't want to be held here.

This concept of true desire emerged again in contrasting themselves to other women whom they did not expect to make it through the center and who were expected to fall back into drugs and crime. When describing the women she expected to fail, Winona stated:

> Most of them are court ordered and don't want to stay clean. They are just clean because they have to be and they will be high as soon as they get out. The only difference with me is that I want to stay clean and there are a lot of other people here that do too.

## Making Change

Beyond describing the claims of change to their criminal or deviant lifestyles, it is important to discover what changes were made and how they were made. Although spiritual conversion, especially among evangelical Protestant adherents, typically is described as a single moment of epiphany, most residents noted that their change was gradual. Failen's account of change provides an organizing concept for this section:

> God works on you from the *inside out* [emphasis mine]. He doesn't do like an extreme makeover on you, you know what I am saying? Let's color your hair and put on some makeup and some new clothes and you are straight, it doesn't work like that. He is going to take you and try to work on you with your dirt on the inside [and] get all them skeletons out of your closet.

### Internal Changes

#### Relationship to God

Using the concept of God working from the inside out as a model, I focus first on internal changes experienced by the women. For many their change was linked to adopting a different view of a higher power. Instead of viewing God as distant and uncaring, Hartley shifted to:

> believing that there's not nothing He can't do. You putting your all to Him, waking up every day praising God that you're here for another day.

In some cases residents admitted that because of their difficult circumstances, they had either abandoned their faith or believed that a higher power had abandoned them. Patricia noted:

I never thought I would have faith again I really didn't. . . . Now it's like I have this awesome relationship with God.

These quotes are illustrative of how women viewed God and how they perceived that God viewed them. This topic has been the subject of several studies of individual attitudes towards crime control and punishment. According to recent survey research, religious adherents who embrace images of God as loving and forgiving are less likely to support capital punishment and other punitive approaches to offenders. Additionally, stronger attachments to religious values of forgiveness are positively associated with favoring rehabilitation and treatment (Applegate et al. 2000). Unnever, Cullen, and Applegate (2005) found that individuals who truly can "turn the other cheek" and are compassionate toward others are less supportive of "get tough on crime" policies. This research demonstrates how views of God may impact both individual identity and attitudes on many issues.

As the women crafted their narratives of redemption and change, they attributed their ability to change to the center's emphasis on religion. In addition, they believed strongly that they would be able to maintain this religious commitment because with "God on their side," they would be able to avoid negative influences and to sustain or build positive influences. Their ability to become new people and to maintain this identity was due to their restored or newfound faith in God, which was fostered by their time at the center. Many of the women made references to how, according to Scriptures, Jesus Christ was able to conquer sin and be raised from the dead. In a similar vein, the women saw themselves as capable of winning their battles with drugs and crime though God's power. Many of the women described this as a process of surrendering to God's will, which involved restructuring their lives around religious activities such as prayer and reading Scriptures. The women believed that by directing their thoughts and actions towards God, they could channel a divine power and successfully overcome their struggles. As Winona said:

The only problem with addiction is that it's sin. So once you get sin out of your life you're okay. And I feel like that's true. You know if you get God, you'll be okay.

It seemed that acceptance of God empowered the women, thus allowing them to join with Him in conquering sin, which for most of the women took the form of conquering addiction to drugs or alcohol.

The women claimed not only that God was a partner in their fight against crime and drugs, but also that He acted as a father figure by offering comfort in times of trouble. For these women the Bible was seen as God's word and was a resource for answers to life's problems. The women described going to God for all matters. This meant not only spiritual matters, but also financial, social, and emotional matters. The most worrisome issue, of course, was the possibility of relapsing into their old way of living. As Talia noted:

> He just seems to answer, you know. He opens doors and answers your prayers.

When asked about the urge to use drugs, nearly all of the women stated that prayer and reading Scriptures helped to take their minds off the temptation to use. As Joley explained:

> Well I mean like I said, you pray, a lot of time I just pray "God please take away this craving," and immediately He will take it away.

The notion of God as all-knowing and in charge of their lives allowed them to believe that He knew their past actions and led them to make real changes in their lives. The women were able to justify past actions because, instead of having to accept the full burden of responsibility, now God held responsibility for their life course. According to Cameron, God had always been there, but she had not acknowledged His guidance for her life until arriving at the center:

> I've always heard God speak to me and guide me through my spirit. At times that I should've listened, I didn't and let's just say I was in the wrong place at the wrong time and consequences happened and now I'm more aware of that conscious. When the spirit tells me, "Don't do that," I pay more attention to it. I listen to it because I know there are major consequences. You know, He's been calling me for a long time and I listened this time. I had to follow that.

*Transition from Old Self to New Self*

As the women created or rekindled a relationship with God, they described the next step in the process, which for them was a change from a criminal identity to a prosocial one. Many investigators have explored the social psychological correlates of crime desistance. Based upon extensive in-depth interviews, Maruna (2001) found that those who desist from crime typically create a "prosocial narrative identity" that can account for why prior criminal actions are not true reflections of their core selves and why their present and future actions have new meaning. This narrative identity integrates shameful life events into a coherent and empowering whole, which then provides individuals with hope for the future. This new outlook is thought to be instrumental in successful crime avoidance and in the promotion of prosocial behaviors (Maruna 2001; Maruna, Wilson, and Curran 2006).

Similar to interviewees from those previous studies, women interviewed at the center tended to redefine their past and current lives in terms of when they arrived at the facility. Most women offered a chronological narrative where coming to the center was the start of a new period in their lives. It was here that their "clock was reset" or their time started over. Throughout the narratives, participants made clear distinctions between the old self and the new self. The women claimed that desistance from crime must include a way to rationalize their checkered past, to address it, and to move forward.

The women did this through the lens of faith by identifying themselves as together now with God and separated from their prior life of crime. Winona reflected on her past and present:

> Well when I first got pregnant, when I found out I was pregnant I stopped using and then I stayed clean for like a month and then I relapsed. Then I went to jail. So I really thank God I went to jail or I probably would have continued using. And I used to talk so bad about people that used drugs when they were pregnant, but I mean I was the same way. But I'm glad I went to jail.

She believed that God planned for her to be incarcerated to prevent her unborn child from being affected by drugs. The women viewed their past wrongs as rebellion against God's plans. They also rationalized previous crimes and deviant acts as precursors to finding faith and healing in a higher power.

For some women at the center, the shift in identity was linked with a change in their view of drugs and addiction. They claimed that addiction was a sinful choice rather than a treatable disease, despite claims by most traditional drug rehabilitation programs. Sarah described how she viewed herself while addicted to drugs and how that view changed during recovery:

> Yes, I definitely was a bad person. And no, I didn't think I was a bad person when I had a "disease." When I had a disease it was like cancer, it was incurable. I was always going to be like this and I was probably going to die an addict because I have this disease but now

I've learned that I was a bad person that made bad choices and that's okay because God's saved me from that.

Thus, the women believed that it was necessary for them to go through drug addiction and all sorts of other negative experiences to find God in the recovery process. Shelby compared her current strong relationship with God to a time when she deliberately tried to avoid religion:

Well it is different than anything I have ever experienced before because it's a relationship and I'm trying to get to know Him better and become closer with Him. Basically you do that by praying and reading the word of God and giving thanks to Him. Whereas before I said I didn't feel like He was there, well now I feel like He is here all the time because I am actually bridging that gap. Before I was trying to stay away, but now I know He is there. I feel His presence.

Believing that God was in control of their lives and the lives of people around them gave the women at the center a sense of security and confidence to move forward in recovery. The women believed that by allowing God to guide them on the road to recovery, they would feel less burdened by the stressors of everyday life. The support that they felt God provided was a critical coping mechanism for continued success in drug rehabilitation and the ability to transition smoothly to the outside world.

The women's journey to the point of envisioning a new self varied in two ways. Many acknowledged that they wanted to "be clean" for a while, while others admitted to trying but then having a relapse. One common reminder conveyed by the administrative staff and volunteers was that "the center is not a rehab." Their explanation was that treatment is a long-term process meant to address all aspects of life in the context of faith, and not a stereotypical one-month rehabilitation stay. Many of the women who experienced other treatment programs used particular aspects of the center to differentiate this time in recovery with the other treatments that ended in relapse. Some women, such as Gladys, noted the center's policy on allowing family members to stay at the facility under some circumstances. She stated, "It's not like other treatments when you're in seclusion and you can't see family." Most of the women, such as Joley, placed primary importance on the faith-based aspects of recovery:

I was struggling with getting clean and sober and I kept going in to detox centers. My doctor was detoxing me on phenobarbital and then I would be high or drunk again within two weeks and I just kept going back to the doctor again and then went through severe withdrawals and everything with that and he felt bad for me. He is a Christian doctor and he is also a Christian that had always shared his faith with me. He said it is obvious you keep doing the same thing and going to these programs and they are not working for you. He said, "I don't think you're going to get sober and stay sober until you put God first in your life." He said, "I think you should go somewhere like the center."

Delia contended that: "You have to have love, patience, and humility, and that's something you have to have in everything you do." Although these attributes may have a spiritual root, residents came to view them as important apart from their faith. Keira provides the summary of the broader changes she experienced while at the facility. In doing so she provides a clear juxtaposition of an old and new self:

I know I have a purpose in life now. Before, I thought I wasn't worth anything anymore. Basically, just lost my drive in life. . . . I was still a parent that was there but I wasn't the parent I wanted to be. You understand what I'm saying? I had dealt with a lot of health issues too and struggled with that. So now just with getting my medication and stuff corrected, and getting my relationship with God back in order. My relationship with my family has never been better. You know, all around just everything is better.

Others claimed that the center helped them to adopt a different perspective that prioritized God and others. This was an important part of the identity transformation process, because most of the women admitted to struggles with selfishness and self-centeredness. Candice summarized her old and new approach to living:

Well, for me, I knew about everything, but I was only living for me and my addiction. Once I opened myself up in here with what they were trying to drill in me with every class that I took was that if I didn't change my heart then it didn't matter because I wasn't going to be able to keep my sobriety unless I become a different person. So I started praying to God and eventually it was like I had a real relationship with him. Once that happened I just felt like a different person, I know that I'm not the same person I was when I got here.

Similarly, Ursula noted a "change of heart" that was linked with a change to a more prosocial identity. She reflected on moving gradually from her old self to a new self:

I was hateful. I hated everyone and I can't say I'm completely over it, because I've only been here three months. But now I walk around smiling and talking to everybody. It's definitely softened my heart I guess you could say.

## Self-Worth and Self-Respect

As the women transitioned to a new self that was rooted in faith and sobriety, several byproducts of this new outlook emerged. Chief among these byproducts was an increase in self-worth and self-respect. Self-worth encompassed the idea of a positive view of self. The development of a positive sense of self came from an understanding of God's love for them, along with a correspondingly sanguine view of self. In fact, the women believed that developing self-worth and self-respect were essential for them to be successful. For many of the women it had been a long time, if ever, since they had a positive view of self. Moreover, increases in self-worth and self-respect in previous studies have been important predictors of crime avoidance and desistance (Harris 2011; Maruna 2001).

The development of self-worth was most pronounced among women who were still under state supervision or who were previously incarcerated. As Ellen explained:

The center has helped me in so many ways. I feel like I am no longer just a piece of trash. No matter what anybody says to me I know that I am a woman of God now, and nobody can take that away from me.

Beulah described the physical bondage that she experienced while in prison by noting:

I was in bondage within myself. I really hated life. I didn't feel worthy. I felt like I'll never amount to much of anything.

When asked whether this view of self had changed since coming to the transitional facility, she replied, "Oh yeah, I've definitely overcome that. I love me!" Many residents claimed that the facility's slogan, that they are becoming "women of God," gave them self-worth and a sense of empowerment. As a result, the women then felt more in control of their circumstances.

It was striking from the narratives how self-worth and self-respect were in such short supply when women first arrived at the facility. Just over two-thirds of the women interviewed claimed that they did not care about themselves or others prior to arrival. Likely only a handful of the 70 women interviewed could be defined as "healthy" according to standards set by mental health professionals. Avita, who had a lengthy history of drug crimes, noted:

> I've been here over a year and it's taken five relapses and getting kicked out for me to realize that I need to change. So I guess in the last two months I feel myself changing, because I just recently came back.

When asked how she knew she had changed this time given her history of relapse, Avita explained:

> I can feel my heart softening. I'm not as quick to mouth off at someone. 'Cause I had a really bad attitude. I didn't care. I thought the world hated me and I hated the world, so I would just go off on people and it was one of my downfalls. If someone would look at me wrong I would say something. And now it just rolls off my back like water.

For many of the women the root of their increased self-worth was a new understanding of God's love for them. By developing a sense of self-worth, the recovery/desistance process became personal for them. They believed that their goal of crime desistance was now a concrete one, and was something they needed to accomplish for their own well-being. Jasmine stated:

> If we were able to get clean by ourselves, we wouldn't have damaged our health like we did. It's not enough. Doing it [getting clean] for somebody else makes it worthwhile [only when] you start to value yourself.

This quote underscores the internal struggle of changing for self versus changing for others. In the end she claimed that external factors (e.g., family, friends, economic factors) could motivate change, but that a positive view of self had to be paramount in the change process.

For others, the increase in self-worth was rooted in how they were treated by staff members and volunteers. Most interviewees housed at the facility for more than a few months described the center in intimate terms such as "community" or "family." Jewel said:

> I like the way that the center builds your worth. They give you chances even though you're a convicted felon. Even though they're afraid you might steal their equipment, they give you a chance to prove who you are and what you can do.

Jewel's quote references her work assignment at the center where she operated expensive media equipment for religious services, educational classes, and special events. Trusting her to operate this equipment despite her lengthy criminal history seemingly was a major boost to her self-worth.

Once they began to develop self-worth, they wanted others to view them similarly. For others to adopt the perception of them as reliable and recovering offenders, their actions had to match their newly developed sense of self. For most, the belief that God loved them despite their past problems became the catalyst for their own decisions to leave the criminal lifestyle. Celeste summarized it this way:

> You know, you can't fool God. I know this. And my day to leave here is XXXX and I asked Him—he knows what you going to do before you do it. So I asked, I just got to keep pressing on and keep believing and keep asking him to keep me strong. And He will, if I sincerely mean it. He will. Yeah, I got to sincerely mean it. He give you chance after chance after chance, I know this. But He loves you unconditionally.

Once the women embraced the idea that God's love for them was unconditional, the concept of going straight became possible. They also described how the kindness and support from staff members and volunteers at the center gave their lives a greater sense of intrinsic value.

*Forgiveness*
Another emergent theme from the narratives was that the women believed forgiveness was the gateway to establishing better relationships with those around them. Forgiveness came in three forms: (1) forgiveness from God, (2) forgiveness of self, and (3) forgiveness to and from family and friends. Forgiveness from God occurred first for the women and led typically to forgiveness of self. Talia stated:

> I think the main thing the center has done for me to repair my relationships is show me that I can be forgiven and that if God can forgive me, I can forgive myself because that's the hardest thing I had the problem with.

The women believed that God was the ultimate source of power and that if He was able to forgive them, then they must be able to forgive themselves as well. Many of the women did not want to disappoint God, and by forgiving themselves, it moved them one step closer to developing a new self that was law-abiding.

After the women forgave themselves, they claimed that forgiveness to and from others was the next step in their transformation. This was an informal process and was not one mandated by the center. Contacting individuals whom they had wronged was not required as it might be in many twelve-step programs (e.g., Alcoholics Anonymous) or in various treatment facilities. Nevertheless, this was a difficult process for many of the women because of years of problems, abuse, hatred, and disappointment in their prior relationships. Winona, an addict who started using drugs with her mother when she was just age 14, described the difficulty in forgiving her mother:

> Well, being in the same building with my mom has been hard for me. I mean at first it was why I came here and then a lot of feelings came up where I knew that I really hated her and I had to deal with forgiving her. And you know, I just kept saying that I don't feel it, I don't feel it. I hate her. I hate her. But forgiveness is a choice and that is the biggest thing I have learned since I have been here.

With only a handful of exceptions, the women chose to forgive others for the pain and problems they caused as a way to overcome their past. To move forward and to rebuild those relationships, the women believed they had to forgive the people in their past. Sometimes, however, rebuilding relationships was not an option. Not only did the women need to forgive themselves and others, they learned to humble themselves and ask for forgiveness from the people they hurt. Julianna described the good and bad outcomes of asking for forgiveness:

> Well, my Mom, she's not here. My Dad, we're building our relationship back up. I mean, it's fine. He forgave me, he's okay with me. My family loves me. I have a really good family. They've forgiven me and accept me and everything. The other ones, I've just forgotten and left them out there where they were. I have to pray for them but there's nothing else I can do.

Progressing into their new prosocial sense of self meant reestablishing relationships with positive family and friends that were lost previously. The women acknowledged that this was a tricky task, because they had to sort out the positive family and friends from the family and friends who contributed to their criminal lifestyle. Even when they could identify positive influences, forgiveness was difficult because of the hesitation expressed by family and friends that did not want to be hurt or disappointed again.

*Purpose and Hope*

A final byproduct of the creation of a new self was that many of the women at the center expressed the belief that God had a specific plan and purpose for them. They believed that the adversities they experienced were a part of God's master plan for their lives and had meaning. The women believed that God's purpose for them included these struggles so that they could get to the place that they needed to be in their lives. Attempting to find God's purpose in their adversities allowed the women to be reflective and to reevaluate their criminal past and all of the progress that they had made. Through this progress, confidence and hope for a more stable future emerged as the women trusted in the plan that they claimed God had designed for them. Marisol explained that her life experiences and challenges were not in vain but that God allowed these things to happen for a reason. She seemed reassured and hopeful about her present and future because God had control of it:

> Sometimes God puts us through things. . . . He won't put more on us than we can handle. I know He had His hand on me, keeping me safe while I was going through the storm. I promise you when He pulled me out and sent me here, He had a plan, so that's what keeps me very optimistic.

Amazingly, the women claimed that despite the many horrible situations in which they found themselves—such as prison, drug addiction, domestic violence, homelessness—all of these situations were part of a "divine plan" that would end well for them. Most women interviewed at the center were convinced that God allowed them to endure all of their hardships and addictions so that they could help others. Joley wanted to use her experience with drug addiction to help others who were facing addiction by becoming a peer counselor. She argued that she could "turn my test into a testimony" and thus be an inspiration to others experiencing what she had overcome. Joley believed that God had a purpose for her from the beginning and that He wanted her addiction to be used to make a positive impact. She felt that God allowed this experience so that she could help recovering addicts.

> Well, I mean I have always been interested in psychology and addiction, being an addiction counselor. . . . I know that you aren't going to listen to somebody who hasn't been down the same road that you have so who is better to reach somebody who has been there, you know, been down that road then somebody was has been there done

that. So, I figure I can use my testimony, my experiences to help other people who struggle with the same problems.

By identifying a higher calling or vocation for their lives, the women believed that they were valuable and had a purpose in life. For many this was the first time they felt such a purpose. By having tangible purposes and goals, the women felt a sense of importance and to them, the value of staying crime- and drug-free was greater than ever before. The women thought that since God had blessed them by delivering them from their struggles, they, in turn, were encouraged to help others in any way possible and to allow themselves to be "instruments of God." Julianna hoped to do this through her job at the center: "I just want to give what God's given me." By this statement, Julianna expressed her gratitude for her recovery, which she claimed was possible only through God. She wanted to use the opportunities that she believed she was granted because of God's power to help other women to stay off drugs, to stay out of prison, and to get stable jobs and families.

The women also believed that their recovery would be successful because they thought that with God, all things were possible, including overcoming their many struggles. Hope gave the women confidence that they would recover successfully from drug addiction and go on to live meaningful lives. They said that this was possible because the women believe that they have God to depend on and to help them as they follow the "straight and narrow path." By having a higher power in their lives, they were confident that they would be successful and not return to prison or a transitional facility again. Kelsey's summary is illustrative:

> As far as myself today, I'm going to stand firm on the word of God, and I know that if I use it, use the word of God then that's the only offense weapon there is, the rest are defense weapons. I know the sword of the spirit is the word of God and I know that if I use that to fight these principalities and darkness and all this kind of stuff, I'll overcome.

## External Changes

### Religious Activities
When asked how the center played a role in the claimed change to a prosocial identity, residents routinely attributed it to the faith-based classes, chapel services, and small-group Scripture studies. The women described a time when they became deliberate about religious activities such as classes, services, study groups, and prayer time. This is not

surprising given the overarching emphasis on religious transformation at the facility. Keira claimed that attending religious classes taught her the primacy of a relationship with a higher power. She noted:

> The center is who helped me to understand how important it is for my relationship with God. And, how to be a healthy functioning, living adult.

Carrie added that the faith-based programs:

> help me keep my connection with God. [That] keeps me on my toes. That and reading my Bible and studying the Word.

The majority of residents described the faith-based approach of the facility as saturation. Roberta explained life in the facility in this way:

> This place helped me, yeah, because all they talk about is a spiritual program and all you hear when you walk around the hall is Christian music all the time. And the classes [are] spiritual and the people that come talk to us and the people that do the classes, they talk to you and break it down to you.

Lydia reported a similar experience:

> Always you learning about the Bible, you know, you always learning about the Bible. You can walk around and you gonna learn about the Bible, but then you're learning about yourself and other people and how to treat people. And you learning how to be a successful person after [you leave] this place and they tell you little things in that the Bible that, you know, correspond with your life.

In addition to the religious classes and services offered at the facility, many of the women also reported involvement in informal religious activities or activities at other places. Ally summarized her activities:

> Well, since I've been back up here, like I said, I've been trying harder about making sure that I do my own things with God. Spending time with God, you know. Like, when I first woke up. And it's important to me because I know that we're made to do a lot of things here. It's mandatory for us to go to church. It's mandatory for us to go to classes. It's mandatory to do certain things and so I wanted to make sure that I could do these things that aren't mandatory. So, I started to do my own little Bible studies myself, pray by myself in my room, and my good friend . . . me and her go to a Bible study outside of the

center at a girl's house here in XX. . . . So I do recognize the importance of doing things myself outside of the center and I am making an effort to do that.

Thus, the women outlined how faith-based activities gave them a sense of purpose and provided religious content useful in creating the new prosocial identity that they claimed to pursue. In this sense the internal and external changes coalesced and were mutually reinforcing.

*Structure*

In addition to the intended consequence of spiritual development and maturation, the women noted that the religious activities had the additional benefit of providing them with a sense of structure. They claimed that structure was important for regaining control in their lives. Their discussion of structure had two dimensions: daily routine and religious practice. During their time on the streets prior to prison or coming to the center, the women described staying awake and high for several days in a row and then sleeping for several days. A consistent daily routine did not exist for these women during their time spent indulging in crime and drugs. Upon arriving at the center, the women were required to attend devotions in the mornings, to complete educational classes throughout the day, and to secure at least part-time employment. Cameron explained how she adapted to this schedule:

> When you first get here, you don't want to do this program. I'm just going to be honest, you don't feel like going to class, you don't feel like going to church every time. But once you get into the routine of it, you're waking up on your own, you don't have client reps knocking on your door to get you up. I mean for me, I can't answer for everybody else. But for me, I get up before devotion. I'm in the routine so it's basically getting me back to being normal.

Getting a routine established was helpful in the recovery process for these women because it normalized a small portion of their lives. After the women maintained a daily routine, their time was filled with activities, work, and devotion. With this daily routine, they concluded that there was no time left for crime or drug use in their lives and that this structure could be maintained even after leaving the facility.

Beyond establishing a daily routine, the women claimed that developing a spiritual structure was just as important. This included thinking and living in more of a godly than a worldly manner. The center provided classes that promoted the idea of addiction as a spiritual disease and once the women adopted this line of thinking, they were able to incorporate a more Godly view of their choices. Jacie stated:

> Like the class I just got out of, The Heart of Addiction, which is a faith-based class about addiction but it is spiritual and a God-based approach to addiction instead of the secular worldview. You know, addiction being a disease. One of the counselors wrote a book [about addiction]. It is based on it being not so much a medical disease as a spiritual disease.

With the understanding that using drugs is a sin, the women interviewed claimed that they had the ability to turn to God for help when they had the urge to use drugs again. The ways that they sought God typically were through prayer and Scripture reading. These aspects became daily activities, and thus gave them a spiritually reliable structure in their lives. Winona described this by stating:

> Well, for a long time I didn't want to read the Bible and I didn't have the desire to read the Bible, but I had to make myself read it so I would want to read it. That's really the only thing and making myself pray every day, at least before I go to bed. I would make myself pray every night and then it would become a habit.

An established spiritual routine in the women's lives provided not only additional daily structure, but also built on their ability to easily turn to God when the recovery and desistance process became tough.

*Accountability*
Beyond the structure provided by the religious programs, the women also noted how they felt a greater sense of accountability to themselves and to others. Thinking back to the previous discussion of renewed relationships, the women discussed how new and restored relationships with positive people on the inside and on the outside had the added benefit of increasing a sense of accountability. To women at the center, accountability meant taking responsibility for their actions and being accountable for the new self that they claimed God allowed them to create. To continue living out the new self, the women recognized that although they could count on God in times of trouble, they also had to take responsibility for their choices. Many of the women felt that going back to drugs and other crimes would be a major disappointment to God. Jasmine explained how this affected her decision making:

I know that if I mess up again that Satan will come at me in every way.
If I mess again, I know, I'll be dead. I'll be looking at God [in Heaven]
and try to explain why I didn't do something with this chance He gave
me.

If in the future they decided to return to a life of drugs and crime, it
would affect not only them and their relationships with family and
friends, but also affect their relationship with God. The thought of
disappointing a higher power who had supported them during their
"rock bottom moments" was viewed as anathema, and thus a feeling of
accountability to God was a significant factor in wanting to stay of out
prison in the future.

Beyond their loyalty to God, the women understood that they were
accountable for their past actions. Caitlyn stated:

I guess I blamed some of the things that I went through on drugs, but
now they teach you that you have to take your own responsibility. We
made that choice to do drugs, no matter what we were going through.

Blaming themselves for their prior crimes and drug use helped the
women at the facility to think ahead to the future. They were forced to
realize that if they got into trouble again, in spite of their newfound
religious commitment, they would be responsible. Julianna discussed
her future recovery process:

As long as I don't step away cause see that's what happens. I'll get out
of here, and I'll do okay for a minute and I'll just gradually quit going
to church. Or, I'll gradually just go visit a friend that used to do it. I
just can't do that anymore.

Understanding their responsibilities was important for maintaining a
new sense of self. The women had established personal relationships
with God and felt that He was the source of strength in their recovery.
At the same time, they also noted the "sinful nature" of drug use. The
conclusion was that the women could no longer cite physical or mental
disease as the cause for their crimes and drug use, but instead viewed
any backsliding as a failure to live up to their new faith-based
commitments.

*New Relationships and Interactions*
A final area of external change described by the residents related to
interpersonal relationships and interactions. For most residents of the
center, their criminal history caused severe damage to familial

relationships with mothers, fathers, siblings, husbands, and children. This is not surprising, of course, and is a common finding from previous research, especially in the case of drug crimes (McIntosh and McKeganey, 2000; Rhodes, Bernays, and Houmoller, 2010). Whether the damage to familial relationships involved trust issues, abandonment, or feelings of shame, the damage was clear from the women's narratives. In general, the women did not believe that they could have repair those broken relationships on their own; however, they believed that God could restore those relationships and help them make a fresh start. Because of their newfound belief in the omnipotent nature of God and the concept of following God's plan in recovery, they claimed that they could begin the process of rebuilding torn relationships with their families. Julianna, who lost relationships with her family because of her drug abuse, explained the reconstruction of some of those relationships. While in this rebuilding process, she realized that she has not been able to fully repair all of the relationships yet but she remained reliant on God to help with those as well.

The women believed that without God and sobriety, the renewal of those relationships would not have been possible. By providing the women with those restored relationships, the women claimed that God gave them additional motivation stay clean. Since the women's previous drug use was often the primary reason for the deterioration of their familial relationships, the consequence of relapse likely would be the same as before. Consequently, the women were emphatic that they were not willing to risk losing the relationships that God had restored for them, nor were they willing to risk the devastation that their family would experience in the event of a relapse or arrest. Talia, for example, claimed that God restored her relationship with her children since arriving at the center. She discussed how the possibility of disappointing them if she started using drugs again and got arrested motivated her to stay clean when she was tempted to use:

> I remember where I was, I remember where I'm at, and I just know what it would do to my kids and how devastated they would be and that's how I choose not to do [drugs] I guess.

Embedded within the search for these new prosocial relationships with family and others, the women described a significant change in their overall appearance, attire, and interaction style. They seemed to believe that to complete the transformation from old self to new self, their change needed to be noticeable by others, even down to how they dressed, spoke, and even the music to which they listened. Quincy said:

When I think of a woman of God I think of [the difference between] secular music and praise and worship music. I think of cursing and not cursing. I think of carrying yourself not trashy. You know, [being] respectful.

Many residents noted a significant improvement in the way they interacted with others. Anya stated:

Now I respect anybody I talk to, because they respect me as well. You got to give respect to get respect. And just before, I would just not even talk to anybody, and if I did I was snappy with them, and just rude. And I see how wrong that was.

Lucy recalled a recent telephone conversation where her change in interaction style was evident:

I called my lil' girl's father the other day and I was like, "Hello, hey, how are you doing?" and he was like, "Um, are you all right?" I was like, "Yeah!" And I said, "Why you say that?" [And he said,] "Because you not hollerin', screamin', and cursin'."

Others observed not only changes in the quality of their interpersonal relationships, but also in the quantity. Felicity, for example, claimed to seek out more conversations with others, especially with those whom she knew were dealing with difficult issues. She said:

My outlook on everybody else's life and what they've gone through, it's just changed. I'm not so stuck up anymore. I'll talk to people because you realize people just need someone to talk to sometimes.

## Maintaining Change

Despite people's best intentions, religious commitment can become less salient over time and fail to foster prosocial behavior. It is not uncommon for people to experience a religious epiphany while in prison or a halfway house, but then backslide and return to the behavior of the old self. Thus, it is important in this last section to understand how the women at the center plan to maintain the positive changes they have claimed. Nearly all of the participants said that they were confident that they would be successful because it was God's will for them to succeed. They did acknowledge, however, that they must take an active role in staying out of trouble. Their primary strategies for staying straight were to avoid negative influences and to seek positive ones. This might seem like a simple recipe for success, but as we will see it is inherently complicated and some might say even irrational at times.

## Strictness and Separation

Residents at the center described their lives as a daily struggle to avoid drugs and crime, and commonly referred to scriptural precepts regarding "separation from the world." Seemingly they viewed the world in terms of good vs. evil or godly vs. worldly. Based upon this conception, the women noted the difficulties of being a woman of God when faced with the seductions of the outside world. It was not as if the women had a cartoonish devil on one shoulder and an angel on the other, but they seemed cognizant, even paranoid at times, about the possibility of falling into temptation.

To assist in resisting those temptations and to maintain their new prosocial identities, the women routinely set very strict standards for conduct, attire, language, and relationships. When asked what, if anything, she tried to avoid, Cordelia answered:

> [Negative] people, places and things. My old people, old places, old things, and old habits. . . . I had a friend in here, on her cell phone she has a song called "White Bricks" that's talking about cocaine. Since I've heard that as her call tone on her phone, I don't associate with her now.

What most of us remember from grade school as the definition of a noun (i.e., a person, place, or thing) appeared to be an organizing concept for all of the potentially negative influences in life. The women described how any person, place, or thing could be a "temptation to fall" and thus the women needed to be very careful in their choices. For Kristen, separation meant cutting off contact with anyone who might have played a part in her becoming addicted to drugs and serving time in prison. She stated emphatically:

> I know not to associate with the people in my past. Well, the abundance of those people in my past. [I] just gotta stay focused.

Upon first inspection, the strict personal standards claimed by the women might seem overly rigid or even fundamentalist. Nevertheless, the women contended that the strict standards were necessary to keep them from "backsliding. They believed that if they let their guard down even for a brief period, they might return to a criminal lifestyle and/or drug abuse. Their explication of strict religious standards is consistent with the well-known work of economist Iannaccone (1994) in his description of "Why Strict Churches Are Strong." Iannaccone found that strict behavioral standards in small fundamentalist congregations often foster a stronger sense of accountability, identity, and cohesion than congregations with more open and malleable standards. The risk that parishioners take in terms of being defined as outsiders and in reducing their potential web of social networks is rewarded by establishing social support within a small group of like-minded others.

Along with these strict behavioral standards, some of the women had the mindset that they not only avoided negative influences, but also refused to even think about negative things. Meredith provided a unique framework for maintaining a faith-based identity as she faced temptations. She stated, rather forcefully:

> I don't even speak death. I don't do it. I'm gonna accomplish my goals. That's speaking that life thing, you know. You don't speak death. I'm not gonna start getting that doubt in my head. No, ma'am. I'm gonna succeed. I'm gonna reach my goals, and that's all I have to say about that.

Kristen shared a similar approach, even using some of the same terms:

> One thing I learned is how important your tongue is. I'm still learning to say things a certain way that I want to say them, but if you speak life you bring life, if you speak death, you gonna bring death. And I'm trying to learn to only speak life, and I know I'm gonna have a bright future.

It was clear from these quotes that the women were so focused on their faith and newfound commitment to crime- and drug-free lifestyles that they would not even entertain the possibility of another arrest or relapse. Whether this is a sustainable plan for the future is questionable, and will be discussed in the final chapter.

### Social Support

The other side of the coin observed from the narratives was the importance of associating with the right people. As is typical among evangelical Protestants, women from the center placed a strong focus on surrounding themselves with religious others. They believed that if they could surround themselves only with other women of God, they would be less likely to return to the facility or to prison. Residents discussed their desires and attempts to rekindle dampened relations and to develop new ones with like-minded others who could provide positive support and encouragement. Asked her plans after leaving the center in a few weeks, Felicity said:

> I need a support group. And I wanna make sure I find the right support group [after I leave]. I don't wanna fall back into wanting a man to live with and stuff like that, but I think the center has helped tremendously.

Clearly most of the women recognized that they needed the support of others if they were to keep on the right track in difficult situations. The narratives suggested that the women relied on various social support mechanisms to keep themselves focused and inspired. In particular, they found it helpful to seek out assistance from positive others and to increase their social networks. Felicity described the inspiration derived from interacting with women who faced similar struggles:

> It was cool to see people, [then] you know you're not the only one that's been through this. Cause that's kinda how I felt. I felt like, you know, you start feeling like, God why'd you let this happen to me? But other girls have been through it too. So it was nice to see that.

By contrast, Carrie and several other interviewees noted that most of their positive connections were made with staff members and local volunteers at the center. She observed:

> I'm more friends with the staff people here that's been here longer. I guess it's kinda a good thing cause if you hang with the wrong people here just like anywhere else you're gonna get in trouble.

Seemingly there was recognition of the need for social support mechanisms both inside the facility and outside the facility after release.

The women described how social support was in ready supply not only in general, but in particular when they experienced trying situations. Beatrice recounted the uplifting nature of fellow residents during times of sadness and depression:

> The other day I was just so sad. I was depressed and cryin' and every time I turn around somebody tellin' me you're gonna be okay, you just pray, just to have hope and faith. I mean, that helps you out a lot.

Ulga described how others helped her during difficult times:

The faith and the support with faith. With somebody coming up to you and knowing the Scripture that will probably relate to what you are going through. Or just sit down and praying with you.

## Summary

In this chapter I examined the contours of faith from the perspective of women in a halfway house. The narratives of 70 residents provided fascinating insights into coping with a different correctional context. The women at the center believed that after establishing a relationship with God, they could successfully complete the recovery program and maintain a clean lifestyle. They saw God as a guide for leading them through the difficult aspects of recovery that would otherwise be too complicated and difficult to overcome. They believed that establishing a relationship with God made their recovery manageable because it allowed them to make specific changes in the ways they saw themselves, interacted with others, and carried out their daily lives.

Specifically, they claimed that faith provided them with positive internal changes such as a stronger relationship with a higher power, a transition from an old self to a new self, a heightened self-worth and self-respect, the ability to forgive (themselves and others), a purpose in their lives, and a newfound hope for the future. They also claimed that faith provided clear external benefits as they became involved in religious classes, services, and groups. Those religious associations then facilitated a structured lifestyle, a system of accountability, and a means of reconnecting with prosocial family members and friends. The women also outlined strategies for maintaining positive change and for leaving the criminal lifestyle.

As discussed throughout, key themes in this chapter have important conceptual and theoretical implications. Chief among those is the theme of "dramatic self-change" (Athens 1995). Whether the result of some life-affirming event or a response to hitting rock bottom, women at the center claimed that they reached a point where the process of dramatic change began. For most this change was away from a life of drug addiction and crime. I should be clear that even though the change may be portrayed as dramatic, it is the beginning of a process, and not an end result. Athens describes the process of change this way:

> Our histories of dramatic self-change read like an open book. We start a new chapter of our lives each time we undergo dramatic self-change. The fragmentation of a previously unified self marks the end of one chapter and the beginning of a new one. After successful passage through the fragmentation, provisional, praxis, consolidation, and

social segregation stages, a new self is created to replace the old one that fragmented. (1995, p. 584)

Indeed, change is a lifelong process and may need to be repeated multiple times in life. As Athens (1995, p. 584) noted, "The final chapter of our lives can not be written until after our death."

The themes I found here are also consistent with the work of Giordano (2002). In her work on cognitive transformation, she highlights the shifts that facilitate desistance from crime. It is important to note that she studied unique factors in change for women offenders, which had not been explored fully in previous studies. She found that "women were more likely than men to describe religious transformations and to focus heavily on their children as catalysts for changes they had made" (Giordano 2002, p. 1052). She also found that many "women who were more successful as desisters crafted highly traditional replacement selves (e.g., child of God, the good wife, involved mother) that they associated with their successful exits from criminal activity" (Giordano 2002, p. 1053). In this chapter I expanded Giordano's work by providing a more comprehensive view of how religion may serve as one of the hooks for change in the desistance process among women offenders.

Finally, the work of Maruna, Wilson, and Curran (2006) is important here as well. Consistent with their findings, the new faith-based identities of women residents at the center may be associated not so much with being a certain type of person, but with engaging in an ongoing spiritual struggle. This perspective may illuminate the concept of being born again and may make sense of how identity work and evangelical Protestant traditions help individuals transform from an old self to a new self. Stated another way, the women at the center are not claiming necessarily that they are finished being transformed, but that they are better prepared for the ongoing struggles of their lives. Thus, the mistakes of the past are recast as part of a spiritual struggle that will continue for the rest of their lives.

# 8

# Returning to the Free World

In this penultimate chapter I examine how prison inmates and residents of halfway houses think faith will help them as they return to public life. To explore this issue I draw from 173 in-depth interviews. As noted in the Appendix, these interviews were conducted in a men's prison, a women's prison, and a women's halfway house in the states of Alabama and Mississippi. There was unanimity among the interviewees that they made (or were in the process of making) positive changes in their attitudes and lifestyles. Thus, there are two key questions to address now. First, what factors do the interviewees cite as primary motivations for maintaining that change once they are released? Second, what strategies will the interviewees use to maintain that change and to avoid a return to some form of community supervision? Simply put, what are the motivations for going straight after release and what are the plans for staying straight?

Before discussing the narratives, however, it is important to set the proper context by summarizing the literature on prisoner reentry and perceptions of life after release. As summarized in the first chapter, for the past four decades the criminal justice system in the United States has been on what Austin and Irwin (2012) called an "imprisonment binge." The current incarceration rate is nearly 500 per every 100,000 residents, which means that about 1 in every 200 residents is behind bars (BJS 2012b). One of every 33 adults has been under some type of correctional supervision—such as jail, prison, probation, or parole—at some point during the life course (BJS 2012b). And according to the best-known recidivism study, over two-thirds of inmates released will be rearrested within three years. This "get tough on crime" policy has come with a significant price tag in terms of system expenditures and damage done to individuals and to their local communities.

Although the prevailing approach to the incarcerated from policy makers has been to lock them up and throw away the key, the reality is that nearly 95 percent of all inmates will return to their local communities at some point. Approximately 600,000 inmates are released from prison each year, so this works out to over 1,600 individuals released back into their local communities per day. The pressing question now is this: what happens to them after release?

In her well-received book, *When Prisoners Come Home*, Petersilia (2003) provides perhaps the most comprehensive and detailed description of the struggles faced by ex-prisoners. She analyzed prison data at the state and federal level and conducted dozens of in-depth interviews with current and former inmates, as well as prison officials. In doing so she identified several major challenges faced by inmates as they prepare for and enter what inmates at Parchman and Tutwiler affectionately and longingly called the "outside."

The first major challenge for inmates is the limited support/assistance available from the criminal justice system. Due to the overwhelming prison population, the bulk of funds is used to cover the living expenses of inmates. Because of this, many rehabilitation programs have been eliminated and public support for such programs has dwindled. The typical prison in the southern region offers little more than basic GED and college credit courses, along with a few vocational programs.

Particularly perplexing is that in many men's prisons, inmates receive training for occupations in which they cannot or are not likely to work upon release. In New York, for example, prisoners can take vocational classes to become barbers, but upon release they cannot practice this craft legally because of a state law barring them from obtaining a barber's license. This is just one glaring example of how some prison programs may not be particularly effective in preparing inmates for release. What this means, of course, is that the average ex-prisoner leaves with only a modicum of training and preparation for reintegration into the labor market. Moreover, states typically turn out inmates with a bare minimum of physical resources to start their new lives. In Alabama, for example, those released from prison are given two changes of clothes, $10, and a bus ticket to a destination of their choice.

Besides the limited investment in prisoners while they are incarcerated, parole and supervision services after release have decreased significantly as well. The parole system originally was divided into two parts: parole boards who determined whether prisoners will be released, and field services that included parole officers who supervised inmates following release. In the past, parole officers have assisted prisoners with their reintegration by providing counseling services and financial assistance. However, the criminal justice system has moved toward surveillance and monitoring of prisoners and has largely ignored rehabilitation services.

Other areas where help is needed by ex-prisoners are drug addiction and mental illness. Petersilia details how ex-prisoners typically receive few opportunities for drug treatment because of fiscal and ideological concerns of community members. Likewise, ex-prisoners with mental illnesses might receive necessary medications in prison, but upon release the medication stops and the same problems that led to their previous term of incarceration might surface again.

The second major challenge for ex-prisoners relates to employment and community participation. Ex-prisoners, in particular those with felony convictions, have many restrictions placed on employment, obtaining public assistance, obtaining student loans, parental rights, the right to vote, the right to serve on a jury, and the right to run for public office. In fact, ex-prisoners may be restricted from working with vulnerable populations in fields such as childcare, education, nursing, and home health care. Obtaining a good job quickly thus is very challenging, and yet is one of the most important predictors of successful reentry.

The stark reality is that even when they find jobs, ex-prisoners may still struggle. Petersilia points out that in some states individuals who served time for drug felonies must have their driver's licenses revoked or suspended for at least six months after release. According to one recent study, women offenders who are able to get and maintain jobs reported that their wages were not enough to provide for day-to-day necessities. When this occurs, women offenders are then more likely to resort to illegitimate means of economic survival such as selling drugs or prostitution (Olphen et al. 2009).

The third major challenge that ex-prisoners face relates to housing. Without a steady place of residence and family support, ex-prisoners are unlikely to be successful on parole and it will only be a matter of time before they are sent back to prison. Given that many prisoners are far away from their hometown, they may not have the opportunity to make living arrangements prior to release. Moreover, it is clear that most ex-prisoners do not have positive family members with whom they can live after release. For instance, parole officers might not allow ex-prisoners to stay in a family member's home if the relative has a criminal record. This would force ex-prisoners to find their own residence, but they may lack the resources to pay for first and last month's rent on an apartment.

Even community housing may not be viable, suitable, or stable for ex-prisoners according to Petersilia (2003). Government-supported housing facilities are normally overpopulated and have long waiting lists. If the released prisoners have a felony drug conviction on their records, some state laws prohibit public housing agencies from providing housing (Richie 2001). Thus, for ex-prisoners who do not have a stable family home to fall back on once released, they will encounter many obstacles that they simply may not be able to overcome.

The fourth major challenge for ex-prisoners is that even beyond the codified legal restrictions placed upon them, there are myriad extralegal and informal barriers to successful reentry. Petersilia describes in vivid detail the stigma attached to individuals once they are convicted and sent to prison, and how this label sticks with them even after release from prison. Thus, ex-prisoners who committed serious crimes at a young age are likely to face negative repercussions for the rest of their lives. Even when they are legally eligible for certain jobs, ex-prisoners might be passed over for employment opportunities because of the stigma of being an ex-con.

In my view Petersilia (2003) paints a bleak, yet realistic, picture of the landscape that will be inhabited by ex-prisoners. She comes to the conclusion that the correctional system in the United States is doing little, in fact, to correct anything. From her perspective the correctional system, at least as it functions currently, seems only to further punish and inhibit ex-prisoners once they are released.

## Prospective Studies of Prisoner Reentry

Most studies of prisoner reentry, whether for men or women inmates, rely on retrospective surveys or in-depth interview accounts from former inmates. While this is understandable, it would seem important also to explore the prospective accounts of future freedom from current inmates. Thus, rather than offer post hoc explanations of "what went wrong" or "what went right," I will explore the expectations for successful community reentry among individuals currently in prison or in halfway houses.

One of the only prospective studies of prisoner reentry was conducted by Severance (2004). She sought to understand the concerns that women inmates have when released back into the community, as well as the reentry process more broadly. To do so, she conducted 40 in-depth interviews with women inmates who were classified according to three groups: (1) newly admitted inmates, (2) general population inmates, and (3) inmates approaching their release date. The major areas of concern for the inmates when being released included employment and education, relapse and recidivism, children, food, clothing, and shelter. In addition to the stigma of having a criminal record as discussed previously in Petersilia's (2003) work, several other concerns arose about obtaining and keeping employment. Some inmates were concerned with changes in technology that occurred while they were in prison. By being locked up, some offenders felt that they would be unable to "catch up to the current way of doing things" following release (Severance 2004).

Age was also a factor that worried the inmates. As they grew older, they felt less confident in their ability to gain employment in a competitive labor market. For most they relied on job connections through family or planned to enroll in a reentry program where they could be placed in a job. To escape further involvement in crime, inmates claimed that they would use avoidance strategies such as staying away from old friends with whom they got into trouble previously. One inmate serving time for a drug-related offense predicted, with a hint of sarcasm, that because she would not have any money, it would be much easier to avoid buying drugs.

In regard to the topic of children, Severance found that seeking to regain child custody or visitation privileges could be both positive and negative, depending on the context. For most of the inmates interviewed, they saw their children as motivation to "clean up their act" and to get back on their feet. However, some predicted that the stress of trying to become involved in their children's lives could cause them to return to bad habits such as drinking, drugs, theft, and violence to resolve disputes. Regarding food, clothing, and shelter, inmates relied on significant others almost entirely to help them. One inmate's main focus was on getting a coat to start her transition back into the community. By focusing on such a simple item, this prevented her from focusing on much larger concerns. Aside from the physical and financial needs mentioned, some inmates claimed that faith and prayer would help them once they were released. Simply stated, a few planned to put their future "in God's hands."

## Motivations for Going Straight After Release

At the end of each interview I asked participants about their specific goals after release from the prison or halfway house. The goals mentioned were related mostly to family, education, employment, and connecting with local religious congregations. Unfortunately, the descriptions of their goals were mostly brief and nondescript. It was not uncommon for the interviewees to mention simply getting a good job, finding a good church, or going to school as their goals. When asked for clarification or elaboration, typically they were not very forthcoming.

However, when I asked the interviewees about their motivations for achieving those goals, the narratives were much richer in detail and much more nuanced.

### Family

The most commonly mentioned motivation for change was a specific family member of the interviewees. Not surprisingly, nearly all of those interviewed had family members with whom their relationship had become strained or even broken. This was especially the case for male inmates in Parchman, who were incarcerated in a remote area typically several hours away from their nearest relatives. Beyond the physical distance from relatives, the stigma associated with having a relative in prison, work commitments, the prohibitive cost of travel, and the hassle of passing security and being monitored at the facilities all contributed to difficult relationships and loss of contact.

Although the interviewees listed a variety of family members for whom they claimed to be changing, most of them discussed a young person—such as a child or grandchild—as their primary concern. One resident of the women's halfway house described her motivation to complete drug addiction classes:

> My son. My little boy. Every time I think about it, I'll look at [a photo of] him. Every time I wanna leave, I'll look at him and go, "Well, I'm never gonna get you back if I don't stay and do this." So, I'm doing it. . . . I don't see him a whole lot. I see him two hours a month. And that's through [the Department of Human Resources]. I definitely miss him a lot more. I didn't realize you know, I was taking for granted everything I had. He hasn't really changed. He's become a little bit quieter but he's not even two yet. He hasn't really been affected a whole lot yet.

Sadly, this limited contact with a child still too young to understand the situation was one of the more sanguine stories told by the interviewees. For most, the descriptions of family relationships were much more dire. Another resident of the halfway house described the "tension and heartache" that her drug use caused her family, in particular her youngest daughter:

> 'Cause my kids . . . my youngest little girl . . . she asked me why I did drugs. I said, "Well, baby momma doesn't do drugs no more." She said: "Yeah you do, Momma. You chose drugs over us." To hear that,

when she's five at the time right before she turned six, to hear, you know, somebody say that—it broke my heart.

Besides the physical separation brought on by their incarceration, the interviewees who were also mothers described in great detail the emotional pain of knowing that they had adversely affected the lives of their children and grandchildren. In some ways, this pain seemed to be the most impactful of all their problems. One inmate from the women's prison described her separation from family and how she hoped that things would be different after she was released:

> 'Cause my biggest problem was the last couple years [before incarceration], I hadn't seen my kids because of my drug habit. But I realized in here [prison] my kids and my grandkids want me going back to church. I mean, that's all my kids want is for me to start back in church and start living life [so] that they can be with me and my grandkids again. And that's all that matters. My kids and my grandkids. And God's going to make sure I have that.

Another woman inmate discussed family as motivation to change even though she had a "rocky history" of growing up in foster care and thus having few social bonds. Despite her lack of a stable family life, her goal was to create one for her three children after being released from Tutwiler:

> I have family issues from way back in my past. But I have let it, at one time, just corrupt me and mess me up mentally because I always felt like this. Even being raised up in a foster home, you just feel like don't nobody care. You just don't have nobody. But I think I overcame that, just by talking to the Lord. Asking Him just to give me a peace of mind. Because I don't have a mother and daddy and grandmamma or nothing like this. And they wonder how I still stay sane, you know. I just try to keep myself together, because I guess I'm joyful to have my three kids and I know I'm looking forward to that. I know I have a wonderful life ahead of me.

Inmates from the men's prison shared similar narratives of family struggles and their desire to change those situations as soon as they were released. In doing so they described the same sort of emotional pain as the women interviewees. This inmate from Parchman explains his family situation:

> We [he and his wife] had two children back-to-back before I got locked up. Like I said, I had my business going and all of that. Boy I

can tell you, it is tough being separated from your children and your wife and there is a lot of different emotions I have to deal with now, but I'm older and much wiser. Like tomorrow is the birthday of my oldest daughter and I wish I was there. I get pictures and all, [but] I have to understand one thing—that it was by my own hands and doing so that first thing a person got to realize is you have to come out of denial. Denial is really a destructive force that keeps people from being healed and coming to realize what they have done and that prevents them from being productive in the future.

It is interesting that this inmate seems to have reached a point of self-realization that he caused the family separation in the first place, and that he needed to take specific steps after release to mend the problems.

### Faith

Faith was the second major factor that the interviewees claimed would motivate them to make positive changes in their lives following release. In the narratives about faith and the future, I observed variation across the three sites in *how* faith might help the inmates and residents after release. Just over three quarters of the interviewees (132 of 173) discussed their faith in very general terms and often failed to outline specific applications of their faith to situations in which they would later find themselves. This was somewhat surprising given the way that they described how faith helped them while they were incarcerated. Clearly the discussion of future events might be difficult for anyone, but for inmates and residents who would be released in the short term, it was surprising nonetheless.

Examples of the general discussion of faith for the future were in ready supply from the interviewees. One male inmate who would be released in less than one year explained why he would be successful back in society:

Well, at first it was hard, it was difficult, but now I have set Christ in my life and got closer with Him and [He] draw[s] closer to me. Things are getting more easier. I can see way beyond now. When I couldn't see I was still in the dark, but as He has let his light shine on me, I can focus on the future now more and look ahead instead of looking backwards all the time.

Most of the women at the halfway house, almost all of whom would be free within about one year, discussed the importance of finding a "church home" on the outside, and yet did so in very general and sometimes contradictory terms. Typically the women said that simply staying in church would help them avoid going back to their old ways, but did not articulate the nexus between these two behaviors. One resident described her vision for the future:

> I'll go to church. I mean, stay in focus. Stay in focus. Go to church. I mean, that's my biggest thing, going to church. Going back to church because I used to be at church all the time. Even in my addiction, I was going to church. I hate to say it like this, [but] even in my addiction, I would play gospel music. So He [God] knew my heart but I just had to get back—get right back with him.

This narrative begs the question, of course, if you were doing all of those deviant and criminal activities while going to church the first time, how will church attendance help you adjust successfully to society after you are released this time? From the remainder of her interview, perhaps the explanation is that previously she attended religious services only out of habit or obligation, and somehow she will have a faith commitment this time that will make attendance more meaningful and life-altering.

Other interviewees offered similar generic discussions of how faith would help them in the future. A resident at the halfway house who had been through several 12-step residential drug treatment programs explained why this time she would finally get clean and not return:

> I think this is the only thing that has worked for me long term in all actuality. Because the other, the secular treatment facility, I didn't stay sober. I didn't stay clean and sober. So I just think in my opinion that it's a spiritual problem, not a secular problem. So you can only . . . the only solution is a spiritual solution.

Another halfway house resident shared a similar perspective:

> I'm done with it [drugs], my main focus right now is just following what God wants me to do. . . . He needed me to slow down. He put me in jail and He put me in the center, cause he knew something exciting was going to happen in my life and I was going to be a grandmother, and I needed to be focused and strict and back on track again where I was before, back in church where I can raise my granddaughter. . . . The way I raised my daughter is being in church and showing them what God can do for them. And show them what God has done for me.

The lack of specificity in explaining how faith would help them once they were released was not unique to the women inmates and residents of the halfway house. Male inmates were also adamant that faith would guide them, but it was not clear how that would occur. One male inmate from Parchman who would be released not long after our interview shared this:

> With the help of Christ, all things are possible. So I say, yes, as long as I have God the head of my life, and with the help of his son Jesus Christ, through the Holy Spirit, I can overcome all situations through Christ that strengthen me.

Another inmate from Parchman elaborated on the issue of preparing for release following his second stint in prison. Note how it is unclear why he returned to prison after his first stint, and how things would be different this time:

> The word of God prepares a man and it is very well needed and ought to be productive on the outside. See when I had left [prison the first time], I had prepared. I was prepared and I was able to open my business and do things that I was supposed to be doing. I was able to step up in church and home and raise up to another level of responsibility. I think it is very important that people understand who they are. . . . Like I said we need to hear more and more about love because we are living in a day and time where love is just an emotional thing that people want to turn on and off. People want to use it like a light switch but it really shouldn't be that way. Without love you're not going to care about yourself or anybody else. And the only person that can make you feel good about who you are and to love the next man is the spirit of the Lord. You need to come in contact with God personally.

Thus, as with the large majority of the narratives, there is a discussion about using faith to avoid crime and deviance, but it is unclear how the process works and how the interviewees accounted for their false starts.

### Getting Too Old for the Lifestyle—No More Rock Bottom

A third motivation to emerge from the narratives is the coterminous feeling among the interviewees that they were getting too old to continue a lifestyle that involved drugs and crime, and thus wanted to avoid another time of hitting rock bottom. It is not uncommon for offenders to view their lives as a series of parties and highs, or what Shover (1996, p. 94) calls a life of "ostentatious consumption." That lifestyle, of course, proves quite expensive as often it leads to resource depletion, emotional and physical damage, loss of social relationships, and punishment by the criminal justice system. Thus, as they age and begin to take account of their lives, many offenders reach the conclusion that they are simply too old to continue inflicting the same damage on themselves and others (Shover 1996). In reaching this conclusion there is the underlying acknowledgement that they cannot hit rock bottom again, which in the past may have included drug addiction, serious crime, near-death experiences, and loss of family.

I observed clear evidence of this theme in the narratives of women at the halfway house. About 90 percent admitted to struggling with drug addiction, and about 75 percent of those admitted being in a drug treatment program at least one other time. When asked if she had more motivation to stay clean this time compared to previous attempts, one older resident from the halfway house listed many of the negative things that occurred over time because of her drug use and how she was tired of the negative consequences:

> It's just so many things. It's not worth it. I've lost my kid, I don't have a home, and it's just each time it gets worse. It never gets better. Me and my husband are fixing to lose another car. It's just so many things. Every time it gets worse and I'm getting sicker of it. I want a family. I want a godly family. Like I said, I don't know what the future holds, I don't know what I'm gonna be doing in twenty years, but right now at this moment I want it [to be clean] and I wanna do better. I really do.

Another resident from the halfway house, with a similarly long drug and criminal history, explained that she was placed in a predicament where nothing or no one could get her out of trouble. Although she seemed grateful in retrospect that she hit rock bottom, it was clear that she did not want to return to that state:

> Because I think, back then if I had gotten in a situation where they would have tried to give me like six months, it wasn't enough to scare me straight. It wasn't enough to get my undivided attention. He [God] had to put me in a situation where allowed me to be placed in the situation where money couldn't have got me out. . . . He allowed me to be placed in the situation where nothing could get me moved. Nothing could undo it. And it took me a while to get to the point where I can say I'm thankful for that.

Besides her severe drug addiction and crimes committed as a result, this same woman also had a family member murdered during this time. She reflected on that aspect of her experience:

> And I looked at it like, it could have been me. I used to laugh about stuff, but playing with people is very dangerous. . . . And through the years, the obituaries I had, they just started stacking up. And I just thank God I'm still living and still here.

She seemed certain that if she did not get clean this time, the next obituary in her family would be her own.

Other women at the halfway house were less concerned about matters of life and death, and more concerned about living a "free life" on the outside. One resident claimed that she was finally going to stop using drugs because:

> That's [staying clean] the only option I have. If not, I'm going to be in prison for the rest of my life.

Similarly, a women inmate described her previous experience of being released but then going back to prison, and how she was too old and tired for that to happen again. She claimed that she would do things differently this time when released because her faith was now real:

> I was here ten years ago. And I came through here [and] played. I went to chapel service, you know how you . . . well you don't know. But when I got here, it was just the thing to do—to go to church. Maybe it will help me get out faster. You know, just going through the motions again, just like before. So I didn't really get involved. And once I got here, I ended up at work release. I sang in the little choir there, and I was on the praise team. And I started getting a good relationship, but once you get in a job, and you straight away, so there wasn't time to go to church. So that kind of just dwindled away. And I went home, and once you get free, you just said, "I'm free," and you don't think about going to church. I was going to church, but not actually receiving anything. Just going through the motions of being at church.

What was also particularly fascinating (and puzzling) from the narratives is that the interviewees—men and women, inmates and residents—claimed that although they never wanted to hit rock bottom again, they did not seem to mind that they had hit it at least once before. Intuitively we might think that rock bottom is not only something to fear in the future, but also something to lament from the past. That did not seem to be the case among my interviewees. The overwhelming majority of them claimed that they had to hit rock bottom before real change occurred in their lives. Consider the narratives of these two interviewees, both of whom tried to explain why they and other residents at the halfway house had been there multiple times. They agreed that they had to hit rock bottom for any real change to occur, and they were now motivated to stay out of trouble in the future:

> Because I had hit the total bottom. There was nowhere else to go. I couldn't die. I had nobody, no one, no place to live. I was homeless. I was headed to prison, so I had to look to the Lord.

> I think that some of them hadn't hit bottom far enough, to the point where they were really humbled enough to be able to give everything to God and really take in Christ. I think that I've actually gotten there. I know there's a lot of women that have.

## Strategies for Staying Straight After Release

Having explored the motivations for going straight among the interviewees, the next step is to explore their strategies for staying straight. For those ensnared in the criminal justice system and for those who are free in public life, there is often a major gap between embracing the idea of being a law-abiding, drug-free, and productive member of society and articulating specific strategies for achieving those goals. As I analyzed the narratives it became clear that the strategies for avoiding a return to prison could be grouped into two categories. The first strategy I will call *active resistance*. This strategy involves taking concrete steps to avoid crime, as well as crime-inducing people, places, and situations. The second strategy I will call *passive resistance*. With this strategy, interviewees were hopeful that they would not return to a life of drugs, violence, and other crimes, but they had given little thought to avoidance strategies. In some cases, they refused to consider the possibility that they would return to their old lifestyles and eventually lose their freedom again.

### *Active Resistance*

This was the least common of the two strategies, as just under 30 percent of the interviewees (48 of 173) could be placed in this category. For those adopting this strategy, the tendency was to frame their release date as the start of a new "battle" or "war" against drugs, violence, and other crimes. Often they referred to crime as "evil," "darkness," or even as an "instrument of Satan." It appears that these metaphors were derived from a popular Scripture by Paul the Apostle. When asked how she would avoid returning to the use of cocaine after being released, one woman from the halfway house answered:

> Well, as long as I keep the full armor of God on and stay strong in my faith, you know, in the word of God, friends, talking to somebody about it, praying about it. Those always seem to work.

I asked her to explain what she meant by the "full armor of God," and she completed the war metaphor:

> In Ephesians, Paul talks about putting on the full armor of God. There's the helmet of salvation, the breastplate of righteousness, your feet firmly planted, the belt of truth, and then the sword of the spirit, which is the word of God. That's called the full armor of God [to be used] against the devil's attacks.

Similarly, an inmate from the women's prison, who struggled with interpersonal violence for most of her life, used the war metaphor to describe how she would try to avoid arguments that in the past led to fights and then to arrests:

> I have learned, because Proverbs talks a lot about "The wise one keeps her mouth shut, the fool wants to speak." So I have learned to keep my mouth shut. Because sometimes my opinion doesn't really matter. And if it's really, you know, what is it about the war and the battles? Choose your battles because the war is to come.

For many interviewees the focus was on using prayer and Scripture reading to avoid temptations. One male inmate from Parchman outlined how he was able to stay out of trouble while in prison, and he claimed that the same strategy would be effective after his release:

> Some mornings I just want to feel like I might just say: "F the world. I don't like it here." So, I like get up, get along with everybody. Like this, see what I'm saying, right here [holding up a Bible.] Everybody just needs to read they Bible and you have a better piece of mind. So you wake up in agony, you wake up you need to start praying, you may wake up in the morning and start praying. You feel better. If you wake up and don't pray, you might go out step out and get off with somebody right there. See, if you would've prayed you ease more. . . . See, if you pray and mean it, you feel it. But if you here dying up praying, just bull-jiving, you got some bull-jiving prayer. He [God] don't hear it.

This inmate emphasized the importance of genuine faith and religious practice and claimed that his constant and "fervent prayer" would help him avoid crime. Another woman inmate from Tutwiler told the story of a recent incident to demonstrate how she would handle difficult situations once released:

> Just like today, it was a girl that was in the dorm with me. And she like me in a special kind of way. But I made it plain to her: I like you as a friend. I don't mind getting to know you, we can talk and, you know, carry on. But she had a "wife" she said across the dorm. So that girl over there was getting mad because she was talking to me every day and we'd carry on. She would sit on my bed, you know. . . . And so her wife was saying: "There go your B right there. There go your ho." All that stuff. But I never said nothing to her. I just kept on going. So last night she came to me, she said: "Yeah I'm ready for you now. So and so is gone." And I'm like: "Lord have mercy. Do I have go to the shift officer about this, because I'm going to walk on and I'm not going to fight with her. I'm trying to go home to my children." . . . And so today, she come up the hall and there weren't a whole bunch of people around, but she came in my face, she said, "You have a problem with me?" I said: "Look here, baby. I don't know nothing about you. I don't want to argue with you about nothing. I try to get along with everybody. I'm not going to be in this prison arguing or fighting about another female, which is what we are. Best thing for you to do is try to go home to your kids, like me. You just have a good day."

As part of the distinctive mindset associated with active resistance, the strategy also typically included how to avoid being around drugs and being offered drugs. Because most of the interviewees had a history of drug abuse and linked it with their other crimes, they claimed that avoiding drugs was their top priority. This is not always possible, of course, and so they had to consider how they would refuse drugs when offered. One resident of the halfway house said she would respond this way:

> Oh, I'll call the police. I'll have them arrested. Because I won't tolerate it. I won't have it around me. I mean I'm good friends with the police officers. . . . I don't want it around me, period. I mean, there's going to be some opportunity because of where I'm from. I mean, it's extremely bad down there, but I know how to turn away and walk away.

Calling local police on friends, family, and associates certainly is frowned upon in most local communities, and yet this interviewee seemed willing to risk being a "snitch" to keep drugs away from her. Another halfway house resident described a "free preview" of how to avoid drugs after release. Here she recounted a situation that happened recently when she was granted a weekend pass from the facility:

> Well, I went on [weekend] pass and I had nobody watching over me. The dude that was giving me a ride, he stopped at an abandoned house to go inside and smoke some weed. I didn't know why we stopped, all I know is that I went in there with him. And when he pulled it out I picked it up, I looked at it, I smelled it, I ran it through my fingers, and I took off running from the house. . . . And I stayed strong, didn't go back to the house. I mean, he offered me his [marijuana] and everything, and it just took sheer willpower in me going, "Okay Lord, don't screw up."

From plans to call local police authorities to simply running away from the presence of drugs, the interviewees articulated various strategies to avoid returning to prison. Of the offenders who took this active resistance approach, about one-third of them outlined extreme measures they would take to avoid even being near their greatest weakness. One woman from the halfway house was about to be released after her seventh attempt to recover from alcohol addiction. She explained her response to an invitation for a party that was scheduled just after her release:

> I mean, a friend of mine asked me the other night if I wanted to go to his aunt's birthday party [after release] and I said, "Will there be drinking there?" and he was like, "Yeah." I said no. It's not that I'm going to do it [drink alcohol], but I don't want to see it and have it on my mind. . . . I do everything in my power— ask questions, know my surroundings, and what I'm facing before I go.

In taking these extreme steps of avoiding all locations where alcohol (or any other drug) might be present, there was the tacit admission from the offenders that they had low self-control. Some would even avoid restaurants and stores that sold alcohol, as well as the homes of friends and family members where they suspected alcohol and drugs might be present. One woman, who had been addicted to prescription painkillers, determined that she should not finish her nursing degree after release because of the easy access to drugs. She summarized her decisionmaking process this way:

> Well, I can ask God to show me, [and] close the doors that He doesn't want me to go down. I know I don't need to go back to nursing school and I know I don't need to go back into those fields. I know that

totally, and I know that He's going to guide me in the directions that I need to go.

The crux of the active resistance approach is that the religious individuals create specific behavioral standards and guidelines. In doing so, they are making plans to avoid the pitfalls of drug abuse and crime, and to maintain their freedom once released.

## Passive Resistance

The large majority of interviewees (125 of 173) struggled to articulate a clear vision of how they would avoid a return to their old lifestyle, and most likely a return to prison. Most of the interviewees would soon reenter their local communities with the same (or even greater) temptations as before. Drugs, alcohol, violence, and other crimes indeed would be tempting for them. Given their extensive involvement in formal and informal faith-based activities at the prisons and halfway house, I was surprised by the lack of short- and long-term planning to "fight the good fight of faith."

It appears that there are two key explanations for why the interviewees used the strategy of passive resistance. First, for many it reflected a lack of confidence in their ability to resist temptations and an uncertainty about the future. A woman from the halfway house provided a representative example of this when asked about using drugs again after her release:

> I mean, yes, it's a concern because I have always gone back to it every time. This is the longest I have been clean, so I am really hoping that I don't. I'm never going to say that I will never because I don't think I'm above it. But, I hope I don't.

This crisis of confidence was evident, especially given that she admitted to using cocaine throughout her teenage years, and then using crystal methamphetamine for the past several years. As a follow-up question, I asked how certain she was in her ability to avoid those drugs that plagued her in the past and her timid response was, "probably 85 percent." I did not intend this as a numeric question, but it was answered that way nonetheless. In the context of this narrative, the percentage that she had in mind was probably below 50 percent.

Another woman responded with a similar amount of uncertainty when asked how she would react to being offered drugs after her release:

> I have been there, I've done that. . . . I didn't do them [drugs], but I can't say I didn't do them because I didn't want them. I didn't do them because I am court-ordered and I'm not trying to go to prison, and I'm not trying to go to jail, and I'm not trying to devastate my children. Yeah, it's a scary thought when I'm not here [the center] what's going to happen. And I hope that I am strong enough.

A male inmate took a similarly vague approach in outlining his defense against drugs and crime. Although he appeared to be resolute in his faith, his only resource for resisting temptation was "unseen." Note the lack of any social support or personal decisionmaking processes in this quote:

> There is an unseen person standing here and walking along beside me that is not going to let me slip or fall. And if I do, he is going to pick me up and dust me off and say, "Come on let's try again." Knowing somebody that you can't see is watching over you is a reason to walk that straight line, I guess you could say. I screwed up this life and I don't want to screw up my next one. My next one I want to go up. I don't want to go down.

A second explanation for passive resistance is the "one day at a time" philosophy often taught to individuals in faith-based correctional treatment programs, and especially to those attempting to recover from drug or alcohol addiction. The interviewees from both prisons and the halfway house routinely made reference to this passage from the sixth chapter of the Gospel of Matthew (verses 25–28, 31–34), and so I include it here for context:

> Therefore I tell you, do not worry about your life, what you will eat or drink; or about your body, what you will wear. Is not life more than food, and the body more than clothes? Look at the birds of the air; they do not sow or reap or store away in barns, and yet your heavenly Father feeds them. Are you not much more valuable than they? Can any one of you by worrying add a single hour to your life. And why do you worry about clothes? See how the flowers of the field grow. They do not labor or spin. . . . So do not worry, saying, "What shall we eat?" or "What shall we drink?" or "What shall we wear?" For the pagans run after all these things, and your heavenly Father knows that you need them. But seek first his kingdom and his righteousness, and all these things will be given to you as well. Therefore do not worry about tomorrow, for tomorrow will worry about itself. Each day has enough trouble of its own (New International Version 1973).

As they internalized this concept of "one day at a time" or "not worrying about the future," they did not want to think carefully about or plan how to avoid drugs and crime. Note the response here to the question of concerns about future drug use for a woman at the halfway house:

> Oh, I don't know. Right now I have no concern because I'm at a place in my life that I don't want to [use drugs], and looking around at the people that I have come in contact with here, seeing what it has done to them, I don't want to. And I know I have to take God with me on that part to survive. I know I can't do it without Him, that I do know. I can't do it without Him.

Although she notes that her faith will need to be strong in the future, she does not want to look past the present stage of her life. Another resident at the halfway house was even more adamant that she did not think about the future, about how to avoid negative influences, or about the possibility of being arrested. In a forceful tone, she said:

> I don't even speak death. I don't do it. I'm gonna accomplish my goals. That's speaking that life thing, you know. You don't speak death. I'm not gonna start getting that doubt in my head. No, ma'am. I'm gonna succeed. I'm gonna reach my goals, and that's all I have to say about that.

This approach seemed counterintuitive, especially in light of Benjamin Franklin's famous admonition, "If you fail to plan, you are planning to fail." Given all that we know as criminologists about the lure of crime and the power of social relationships in producing crime, passive resistance may be a risky strategy indeed. It seems somewhat unlikely that at the moment of temptation, people will be able to "just say no to drugs" or other crimes without having considered an exit strategy.

Finally, there are times when categorization is nearly impossible. Although I categorized the narrative from this male inmate below as passive resistance, note how there are elements of both strategies and at times the two strategies appear to coalesce. Clearly this is one of those nuances that is intellectually fascinating, but professionally frustrating:

> *Participant*: I think it is very important and a big step forward not only in your relief but right now. You know because it keeps you stable-minded to make the right decisions. The word of God prepares a man and it is very well needed and ought to be productive on our side. See when I had left, I had prepared. I was prepared and I was able to open my business and do things that I was supposed to be doing. I was able

to step up in church and home and raise up to another level of responsibility. . . . It [faith] helped me totally. It helped to conduct business and raise my family in a Godly manner. It helped me go make groceries in a Godly manner. See it surrounds my life and it would help anybody who grabs a hold of it. I can say personally when I was home operating my business, when I took my eyes off God that's when I started erroring. This is the result of my erroring right here. I started drifting off, hope, misery, and not doing what I was supposed to do for my church. I got so far off track that I didn't even go for that short period and destruction had set in.

*Interviewer*: Do you think you could make it now if you were released?

*Participant*: I can make it now without a doubt because the spirit of fear holds a lot of people down. I no longer have the spirit of fear. God doesn't give me the spirit of fear, he gives me the spirit of sound mind. Again, I stress the love issue because love is what the world was based on. It was what it was built on by God and it would definitely help me out because it has done in the past and has not let me down. I know God won't let me down, I just got to be obedient. Obedient to God and then to man. Because if you are obedient to God then you'll be obedient to man for whatever the situation. Whether you're on the job or wherever you're at, or whoever is giving the orders, you will be obedient to that order and move right in.

## Summary

In this chapter I delved into perceptions of the future among the 173 prison inmates and residents of halfway houses I interviewed. First, I explored their motivations for positive change after release. I found that family, faith, and a combination of getting older and trying to avoid another "rock bottom" experience were the most salient motivators. Second, I explored strategies the interviewees claimed they would use to avoid being ensnared again in the criminal justice system. I found significant variation in how much they thought about and planned for the avoidance of drugs, crime, and negative influences. While the approach of some could be characterized as active resistance, for most the approach was passive resistance.

In their recent commentary on what they call "future selves," Silver and Ulmer (2012) argue that criminologists—and thus the criminological theories they produce—largely have failed to consider how ex-offenders perceive their future behaviors in light of a newly created prosocial identity. The authors argue that, "we view as important the fact that when individuals reflect on why they engaged in this or that behavior or line of action, they usually speak of intentions, desires, hopes, and dreams regarding themselves in the future, whether that future be years or only days ahead (Silver and Ulmer 2012, p. 699).

In this chapter I filled in this hole in the literature by examining how inmates and residents of halfway houses anticipated that they would persist in faith, but desist in crime. Indeed, I found a sharp contrast between interviewees using active resistance versus passive resistance in how they planned to maintain a faith-based identity after release. That is, I found that the future self is dependent upon the strategy chosen to avoid a return to the criminal lifestyle. Silver and Ulmer (2012, pp. 710–711) summarized the importance of this new line of research:

> We suggest that individuals' conceptions of themselves in the future, both desired and feared, are important in part because they motivate the exercise of self-control across a range of situations. . . . Conventional future selves likely foster the development of personal, moral, and structural commitments that motivate self-control efforts. In particular, the process of pursuing lines of action congruent with a conventional future self to which one is personally committed can, over time, produce structural and moral commitments . . . that could further motivate self-control or stimulate efforts to improve one's self-control capacity.

Additionally, there is an important linkage between my findings here and the work of Maruna (2001) on "redemption scripts." Maruna found that offenders in the process of desistance create these scripts to cast their previous mistakes and difficult life situations as part of a larger process of redemption that has a more sanguine ending. The scripts thus create a belief that the reformed offenders are in control of their destiny (Maruna 2001, p. 147). This feeling of control over their destiny is then associated with a major increase in self-agency during the identity transformation and desistance processes.

In contrast to Maruna's study, I found that, overall, the interviewees discussed the future in terms of control from a higher power. As they struggled to avoid crime and drugs many times throughout their lives, they claimed that self-agency was not sufficient to help them go straight. They claimed that control of their lives was limited without the help of a higher power and that faith was their source of autonomy. The inmates and halfway house residents believed that they could not change just through their own will, motivation, or agency, and instead claimed that their redemption script could be written only by a "redeemer." An inmate from the women's prison provided a representative example of this theme:

The Lord is the strength and my redeemer. I need Him. Every step of this thing I'm going through. As I walk on this journey, I cannot step without Him. I can't. It's too much going on.

Finally, regardless of a few "success stories" of former prisoners, the reality of the criminal justice system is that the large majority of narratives end with relapse, recidivism, and hopelessness. I expected fully that the inmates and residents of halfway houses would be optimistic, if not quixotic, about how faith helped them cope with incarceration and would help them after release. Much to my surprise, the interviewees seemed aware that their chances for success back in society were small. Although they may not have been familiar with annual reports from the Bureau of Justice Statistics, they knew that they had only about a one in three chance of staying out of trouble. However, with faith as their guide, these interviewees claimed that they would be among the successful one third.

# 9

# The Future of Faith

After more than a decade spent conducting social scientific research on religion in correctional contexts, often I am asked whether I am a supporter of faith-based prison programs. Putting aside my hesitation as a researcher to admit support publicly for anything, finally, after writing this book, I have developed a coherent answer. The answer is this: I support any correctional treatment program with these characteristics: (1) it has at least modest empirical support (quantitative and qualitative) based on scholarly research, (2) it does not jeopardize the safety and welfare of inmates or correctional staff, (3) it is not coercive, illegal, or unethical, (4) it gives inmates something constructive to do with their time, and (5) its cost is not prohibitive for state or federal governments.

It seems clear to me that faith-based programs in prisons and in halfway houses typically have high scores on all five of these criteria. Even so, my recommendation is not that all correctional facilities create or expand faith-based programs immediately. Instead, I concur with Hewitt (2006, p. 555), who concluded that "Faith-based prison programs give correctional administrators one more element for bringing about change in the lives of inmates held in their care." As one longtime pastor and prison volunteer once told me: "I'm not saying that faith-based programs should be the main course, I'm just saying that they should be on the menu."

## Policy Implications

I have discussed policy implications throughout this work, in particular at the end of most chapters, but I think it is important to recap three major ones here. First, for correctional administrators and staff, my results suggest the need for active prison chaplains and local religious congregants. Prison chaplains might be most effective if they focus their efforts on creating strong social support networks for inmates inside and outside the facility. This may be done via formal and informal religious classes, services, or meetings, but in all cases they must prioritize the establishment of connections between inmates and local religious congregants. Those contacts are likely to provide social support and mentoring for inmates during and after their time incarcerated. As I found in the narratives of the inmates, chaplains sometimes focus just on the individual experience of religious conversion, but the social support mechanisms of faith may also help inmates to create a positive self-image and to deal with the difficulties of prison life. The social support mechanisms of faith, particularly for men, were critical in allowing inmates to remain focused and inspired. The true value of faith for prison coping was in the support and accountability structures it created. Thus, if prison chaplains can create a community of believers, they may well observe more positive adjustments.

Second, as correctional administrators recruit local volunteers to support and mentor inmates, they should search for religious congregants who focus on compassion and redemption, or what was referred to in Chapter 3 as the "logic of mercy." The prison ministry workers I interviewed clearly favored mercy over justice, and thus seemed best suited to deliver faith-based programs. As one veteran prison volunteer emphasized, "Our goal is to preach *to them*, not *at them*." Likewise, it is important that the prison ministry workers avoid the creation of numeric goals, and that they are careful to avoid denominational issues that could distract from sharing their faith and providing encouragement to inmates. I characterized the prison ministry workers I interviewed as having a "simple plan" for their "simple faith."

Third, correctional administrators and staff should be aware of potential gender differences that may influence how they design and implement faith-based programs. I found that male inmates preferred the social aspects of faith more so than the individual or private aspects. Women inmates, on the other hand, claimed that private times of prayer and Scripture reading, as well as staying to themselves, were the best predictors of effective prison coping. The narratives from the Tutwiler inmates I interviewed suggested that the perceived social nature of women diminished the appeal of group religious practice. Although they still wanted social support, nearly three quarters of the inmates I interviewed discussed how difficult it was for the nearly 1,000 women to live together. Consequently, for the women inmates to stay focused on their faith, they claimed that they had to focus mostly on themselves. This finding is in sharp contrast to common stereotypes about women being more social and thus preferring social groups more than men.

## Future Research

My goal with this project was to provide a comprehensive analysis of faith-based correctional treatment programs, yet there are additional avenues for study. Note also that, as with any qualitative study utilizing a nonrandom sample, readers must be careful to avoid generalizing my results to all prisons or to all prisoners. In closing, I want to share three suggestions for future research.

First, future researchers should focus on religious inmates in other regions of the United States and those from different faith traditions. Nearly all of the previous studies, including mine, have focused on inmates from evangelical Protestant backgrounds. The study of inmates from different faith traditions is much needed, not only for the sake of knowledge creation, but also for comparison with previous studies. If researchers could identify a prison facility with well-developed religious programs for inmates of many major faith traditions, it would be an ideal setting for study.

Second, additional research on women inmates is needed. As noted in Chapter 6, to this point there has been little scholarly research on women offenders, especially in regard to faith. My study is intended as a major step in this direction, and I hope that others will follow suit. Future projects could focus on women of different faith backgrounds and any differences in their coping styles.

Third, the only constituency in the creation and delivery of faith-based prison programs not yet studied is the prison correctional officer. Although technically these officers have no role in the provision of faith-based programs, they are on the "front lines" in terms of transporting inmates to and from religious classes and events. Moreover, because correctional officers spend nearly all of their time observing inmates, they are in a key position to describe their informal religious activities, as well as how religion impacts their attitudes and behaviors.

## Final Thoughts

I close now with what I consider the most uplifting quote from the 173 interviews I conducted at two large state prisons and a halfway house. It is from an inmate at the Julia Tutwiler Prison for Women who had served nearly 20 years and was about to be released. She provided an insightful summary of her God, her faith in God, and how she thought her life would play out after being released:

He's able to do the impossible, so I know, I know He's able to do that. And I have to keep trusting in Him. . . . And I have to keep trusting that He will set the captives free who are in prison. And greater is He who lives in me, than He who is in the world. So I have to fall on those Scriptures and weep and be made to endure for a night, but joy come in the morning. Those Scriptures give me strength to know that there's going to be a brighter day. It's going to be a brighter day. And I'll be soon rejoined with my children and my husband too. . . . And that makes me feel good. You know, I know God. He's up there. He's working this out for everyone.

# Appendix: Studying Faith in Correctional Contexts

Over the past decade I have collaborated with about two dozen faculty colleagues and students to study faith in correctional contexts. Although for the sake of consistency I use a first-person writing style, this book draws from and expands upon several works previously published with others. These include:

Kent R. Kerley, Heith Copes, Alana J. Linn, Lauren Eason, Minh H. Nguyen, and Ariana Mishay Stone. 2011. "Understanding Personal Change in a Women's Faith-Based Transitional Center." *Religions* 2, 184–197.

Kent R. Kerley, John P. Bartkowski, Todd L. Matthews, and Tracy L. Emond. 2010. "From the Sanctuary to the Slammer: Exploring the Narratives of Evangelical Prison Ministry Workers." *Sociological Spectrum* 30, 504–525.

Kent R. Kerley 2009. "Religion and Crime." In J. Mitchell Miller (Ed.), *Twenty-First Century Criminology: A Reference Handbook* (pp. 144–152)

Kent R. Kerley and Heith Copes. 2009. "'Keepin' My Mind Right': Identity Maintenance and Religious Social Support in the Prison Context." *International Journal of Offender Therapy and Comparative Criminology* 53, 228–244.

Kent R. Kerley, Todd L. Matthews, and Jessica Shoemaker. 2009. "A Simple Plan, a Simple Faith: Chaplains and Lay Ministers in Mississippi Prisons." *Review of Religious Research* 51, 87–103.

Kerley, Kent R. Kerley, Marisa C. Allison, and Rachelle D. Graham. 2009. "Investigating the Impact of Religiosity on Emotional and Behavioral Coping in Prison." *Journal of Crime and Justice* 29, 71–96.

Kent R. Kerley, Todd L. Matthews, and Troy C. Blanchard. 2005. "Religiosity, Religious Participation, and Negative Prison Behaviors." *Journal for the Scientific Study of Religion* 44, 443–457.

Kent R. Kerley, Todd L. Matthews, and Jeffrey T. Schulz. 2005. "Participation in Operation Starting Line, Experience of Negative Emotions, and Incidence of Negative Behavior." *International Journal of Offender Therapy and Comparative Criminology* 49, 410–426.

## Research Settings

When I first set out to study faith-based prison programs I followed the approach of previous studies, which involved conducting survey research with inmates. The major improvement from those previous studies was that I administered a survey to a random sample of inmates at Mississippi's largest prison. Much was learned from the analysis of this survey data (Kerley, Allison, and Graham 2006; Kerley, Matthews, and Blanchard 2005; Kerley, Matthews, and Schulz, 2005), but I realized that the project needed to be much more comprehensive than one survey study of a prison population.

For me this meant collecting data from four different contexts, all of which are crucial for understanding the nature, organization, and delivery of faith-based prison programs. The four data sources described in this chapter include: (1) in-depth interviews with chaplains and local religious congregants involved in prison ministry, (2) in-depth interviews with inmates involved in faith-based programs at a men's prison, (3) in-depth interviews with inmates involved in faith-based programs at a women's prison, and (4) in-depth interviews with residents of a faith-based women's halfway house. Before detailing these four data sources, it is important to describe the research settings.

The states of Alabama and Mississippi are appropriate natural settings for a study of religion and prison experiences for three key reasons. First, both states have similar demographic characteristics and cultural histories. Alabama is generally perceived as a poor rural state, but with pockets of significant population growth and economic development in key metropolitan areas. According to 2010 figures from the United States Census Bureau, the state has 12 Metropolitan Statistical Areas (MSAs): Anniston, Auburn/Opelika, Birmingham, Columbus (shared counties with Georgia), Decatur, Dothan, Florence, Gadsden, Huntsville, Mobile, Montgomery, and Tuscaloosa. The state's population is nearly 4.8 million and ranks 23rd in the nation (U.S. Bureau of the Census 2011a, 2011b). The current racial/ethnic composition of the state is 69 percent white, 26 percent black, 4 percent Latino/a, and 1 percent other. The median household income is just over $40,000, and 17.5 percent of residents live below the poverty line.

Alabama's current expenditures for education are over $4.7 billion (ranks 26th in nation) and 82 percent of its residents have at least a high school degree (ranks 43rd in nation). According to 2011 data from the National Center for Education Statistics (NCES), only about 22 percent of its residents have a bachelor's degree or higher (ranks 44th in nation).

Mississippi is often perceived as an extremely rural state with limited economic development. According to 2010 census figures, only 17 of the state's 82 counties are classified as metropolitan and only 5 have the designation of MSA, Biloxi/Gulfport, Hattiesburg, Jackson, Memphis (shared counties with Tennessee and Arkansas), and Pascagoula. The state's population is just under 3 million and ranks 31st in the nation (US Bureau of the Census 2011a, 2011b). Mississippi historically has been predominated by only two racial/ethnic groups. The current composition is 59 percent white, 37 percent black, and 4 percent other. The median household income is about $37,000, and nearly 22 percent of residents live below the poverty line. Mississippi's current expenditures for education are over $3.8 billion (ranks 33rd in nation) and 83 percent of its residents have at least a high school degree (ranks 40th in nation). Only about 19 percent of its residents have a bachelor's degree or higher (ranks 49th in nation) (NCES 2011).

Second, both states have similar incarceration rates and prison systems. Both states routinely are in the top five in the nation for incarceration rates, with each state incarcerating about 900 of its residents per 100,000. Alabama currently spends over $444 million annually on its prison system, and Mississippi spends just over $330 million annually. These prison expenditures have increased significantly over time. In Mississippi, prison expenditures more than quadrupled in the past 20 years. According to data from the Alabama Department of Corrections (ADOC; 2010a, b, c) and Mississippi Department of Corrections (MDOC; 2011), the average amount spent annually to house inmates is about $15,000.

As in most southern states, Alabama and Mississippi operate a large number of state and regional correctional facilities, and the majority of these are located in rural areas. Alabama operates a total of 29 prisons, including 5 maximum-security facilities (Holman, Kilby, St. Clair, Donaldson, and Tutwiler), 11 medium-security facilities, and 13 minimum-security camps, plus work release programs and community work centers. At year-end 2011, the total prison population in Alabama was just over 32,000 (ADOC 2012). Mississippi has three large state-operated prisons and 14 regional prisons. The state prisons, all of which include maximum security units, are the Central Mississippi Correctional Facility (Pearl), the South Mississippi Correctional

Institution (Leakesville), and the Mississippi State Penitentiary (Parchman). At year-end 2011, Mississippi housed about 25,000 inmates (MDOC 2012).

Third, Alabama and Mississippi residents have a long history of participation in organized religion and adherence to cultural values based upon religion (Bartkowski and Regis 2003). According to a 2009 nationally representative survey conducted by Gallup (2010), Mississippi had the highest rate of per capita church attendance in the nation, with 63 percent of its residents attending weekly or almost every week. Alabama had the second-highest rate of attendance at 58 percent (Gallup 2010). Similar nationwide surveys routinely find Alabama and Mississippi in the top five in religious attendance per capita (see, for example, Pew Forum on Religion and Public Life 2007). The large majority of churches in Alabama and Mississippi can be categorized as conservative Protestant. Even denominations such as United Methodist and Church of Christ—considered mainline or moderate in larger cites and in other parts of the country—tend to be conservative in Alabama and Mississippi (Blanchard et al. 2008; Kerley, Matthews, and Blanchard 2005; Kerley, Matthews, and Shoemaker 2009; Kerley et al. 2010).

### Data Source 1: Interviews with Prison Ministry Workers

In-depth interviews were conducted with 30 individuals who were either prison chaplains or volunteers in faith-based programs in Mississippi. All interviewees were involved actively in faith-based prison programs at the time of the interview. To identify chaplains appropriate for an interview, I obtained from the state department of corrections a list of all chaplains in Mississippi's three largest state-run facilities. The facilities were dispersed geographically to approximate full coverage of the state. There was variation across each prison facility regarding the use of chaplains. In some the majority of chaplains were compensated for regular full-time or part-time work, while in others chaplains worked on an as-needed basis for compensation. There were also instances in which prison chaplains worked as unpaid volunteers. Because the purpose of the project was to obtain a wide range of narratives of those involved in prison ministry, all chaplains, regardless of time worked or compensation, were included in the study. I then contacted the director of religious programs at each facility to describe the project and to ask for permission to interview each chaplain. To avoid any concerns about coercion, I then spoke with all chaplains individually to determine their willingness to participate. All chaplains at all three facilities agreed to be interviewed.

Members of local religious congregations in Mississippi who were involved in faith-based prison programs were also invited to participate in our study. Participants for our in-depth interviews were recruited in several ways. First, I contacted the directors of state and local ministerial associations for potential interviews. Second, I contacted the local offices of national-level prison ministry programs such as Prison Fellowship Ministries and Champions for Life. Third, volunteers identified from the first two strategies provided referrals to others involved in faith-based prison programs. Typically the individual received either a letter or telephone call describing the project and a request for participation. Our recruitment strategy for chaplains and local congregants yielded a total of 30 in-depth interviews.

The chaplains and local congregants in our study were very similar in terms of demographic characteristics such as age, race, gender, level of educational attainment, and socioeconomic status. The average age was 47, with all respondents between the ages of 35 and 65. Eleven of the respondents were black and the remaining 19 were white. Five were women and 25 were men. In terms of educational attainment and socioeconomic status, the group average was a four-year college degree and the majority could be described as middle class or lower middle-class.

All 30 interviewees were involved actively in a local religious congregation. The majority of their congregations could be characterized as theologically conservative, evangelical, and Protestant, with most reporting membership in African Methodist Episcopal (AME) Zion, Baptist, Church of Christ, Church of God, Methodist, or Presbyterian churches. Although these denominations can be quite varied in theology, culture, political orientation, and worship style in some regions of the country, in the context of rural Mississippi, they tend to fit well within the conservative Protestant designation (Blanchard et al. 2008). The overwhelming majority attended a local congregation with relatives early in life and reported a religious conversion or commitment between ages 5 and 15. Most had been members of local congregations for their entire adult lives. In addition to their involvement in faith-based prison programs, the respondents tended to occupy leadership positions in their local congregations. Examples of these positions included pastor, minister, missionary, deacon, usher, teacher, and business manager.

Many of the chaplains and local congregants had been or were currently ministers at the churches they attended, which made it impossible to distinguish between clergy and laity. There was also substantial overlap in that several of the prison chaplains also did prison ministry volunteer work in prisons other than those in which they were employed, and some local congregants previously had worked in prisons as chaplains or as correctional officers. There was also variation among chaplains in terms of those who were full-time paid employees and those who were under contract as unpaid volunteers.

The ministry workers were involved in a wide range of activities inside the prison. They had widely varying amounts of training, which ranged from those who received only a briefing prior to entering the prison to chaplains and congregants who earned a formal religious education. There was not a uniform training session required of all individuals before they began their prison ministry work. Religious services were attended by inmates from minimum- and medium-security classifications. Attendees were diverse in terms of age, race, and criminal background. The services were a mix of traditional and contemporary styles of worship used in local religious congregations, and typically included core components of prayer, music, and scriptural sermons. Consistent with the composition of religious congregations in Mississippi, most religious activities in the prison could be characterized as evangelical and Protestant.

The typical activities of chaplains included (1) organizing and conducting formal chapel services one or two times per week, (2) coordinating programs and services with members of local congregations, (3) coordinating visits from national-level prison ministry programs such as Weekend of Champions and Operation Starting Line, (4) overseeing and counseling during "emergency suspensions" that allowed inmates temporary freedom during critical times (e.g., illness, funeral, or marriage), (5) meeting with inmates one-on-one when requested, (6) delivering religious reading materials to inmates if requested, and (7) preparing formal reports for the state about inmate religious participation.

Similarly, the typical activities of local religious congregants included (1) coordinating with chaplains to organize and conduct weekly chapel services, (2) conducting informal prayer, discussion, and scriptural study groups within the individual prison units, (3) coordinating with chaplains to arrange visits from national-level prison ministry programs such as Weekend of Champions and Operation Starting Line, (4) communicating with inmates during visits and via mail or telephone, and (5) delivering religious reading materials. Given their similarities, I treat the 30 interview subjects as one relatively homogenous group of conservative Protestant prison ministry workers.

The purpose of the semistructured interviews was to gain an in-depth understanding of the experiences of prison chaplains and local congregants in their ministry work. In particular, the interviews explored how the workers approached prison ministry, the goals and strategies used in their work with inmates, their perceptions of the impact of faith-based programs on inmates' attitudes and behaviors, and the role that they played in creating social networks for inmates after release. Results from the interviews with the 30 prison ministry workers are presented in Chapter 3.

## Data Source 2: In-Depth Interviews at a Men's Prison

To facilitate an understanding of how men in prison use faith to cope with incarceration, 63 in-depth interviews were conducted at Mississippi State Penitentiary in Parchman, Mississippi. Located deep in the Mississippi Delta region, Parchman, as it is commonly called, is the largest of Mississippi's three state-managed facilities and is one of the largest prisons in the nation in terms of acreage and inmate population. Built in 1901, the facility houses over 3,000 males representing all security classifications, and houses the state's only death row for men. One of the oldest and best-known prisons in the country, Parchman has been the subject of many academic works such as *Down on Parchman Farm* (Taylor 1999) and *Worse Than Slavery* (Oshinsky 1997), as well as fictional works such as John Grisham's (1995) *The Chamber.* Parchman has inspired many singers and songwriters in the blues tradition, such as Eddie James "Son" House and Booker "Bukka" White, who were once inmates.

Inmates interviewed for this study were actively involved in at least one religious program at the prison. At the time of the study, there were three types of religious programs in which minimum- and medium-security inmates could participate. First, inmates could attend formal religious services at the prison's Spiritual Life Center. These services were conducted by staff chaplains and local religious congregants. Although formal in organization, these services typically were contemporary in style of music and message. In a typical week, religious services were held on Saturday and Sunday evenings. A few times per year, national programs such as Operation Starting Line and Weekend of Champions and would visit the facility. Second, inmates could attend informal prayer, discussion, and scriptural study groups that met within the prison units and were led by members of local religious congregations. Third, inmates could attend informal inmate-led prayer, discussion, and scriptural study groups within their own units. These groups generally met one or two nights per week; however, in several units at the facility there were near nightly occurrences. Consistent with the composition of religious congregations in the state, the large majority of religious activities in the prison could be characterized as evangelical, Christian, or Protestant.

Participants for the in-depth interviews were recruited by staff chaplains at the facility. Over a period of one month, chaplains made announcements during regular religious services that volunteers were needed to discuss their involvement in religious programs at the facility. The inmates were informed that all interviews: (1) would be conducted with a researcher not affiliated with the prison or state department of corrections, (2) would be completely voluntary and confidential, and (3) would not result in any special rewards for participation or punishments for declining participation. I then worked with prison staff to schedule the in-depth interviews. A total of 63 interviews were conducted over a 12-month period.

The purpose of the interviews was to investigate inmates' religiosity and how this affected their self-images, ability to cope with incarceration, and incidence of prosocial and antisocial behavior. Each interview began with a discussion of inmates' family and religious backgrounds. They were asked about their experiences with family and religion while growing up and the salience of these two institutions. Inmates were then asked to trace the impact of religion on their lives to their present situation, and asked to describe the experience of being incarcerated and adjusting to the prison context. This section allowed us to delve into the issue of prison coping that is central to prison research. Inmates were also asked how they were able to create and maintain faith-based identities in the prison context. Inmates were then asked about the major factors in adjustment and how they were able to cope with these. They were asked also about the experience of negative emotions and negative behaviors that they may have engaged in. The goal was to assess how religion structured the attitudes and behaviors of these respondents, in particular how religiosity affected their ability to cope with confinement.

The average age of the interviewees was just over 37, and the racial composition was 78 percent black and 22 percent white. The majority of inmates were serving lengthy sentences for serious crimes. The average length of sentence was about 27 years and over half of the inmates were serving time for an index offense, as defined by the Federal Bureau of Investigation's *Uniform Crime Report*. The demographics for the study participants mirrored those of the full prison population. Results from the 63 men's prison interviews are presented in Chapters 4, 5, and 8.

## Data Source 3: In-Depth Interviews at a Women's Prison

To understand faith-based prison programs among women inmates, I conducted in-depth interviews with a purposive sample of 40 incarcerated women at the Janet Tutwiler Prison for Women in Wetumpka, Alabama. This maximum-security facility currently houses about 1,000 inmates, and includes the state's only death row for women. Tutwiler is also the receiving unit for all new inmates, and includes nine dormitories, segregation and isolation units, a medical infirmary, and units for inmates who are pregnant, HIV-positive, elderly, or infirmed.

Inmates at the facility attended a wide range of religious services. First, inmates in the sample frequently attended formal weekly services in the prison chapel. These services were conducted by staff chaplains and volunteers from local religious congregations. Second, inmates also attended more informal meetings such as prayer groups, scripture study groups, and choirs or praise teams. In some cases these were led by local religious congregants, but frequently they were initiated by the inmates themselves and conducted in the open areas of their units. The overwhelming majority of religious activities in the prison could be characterized as evangelical, Christian, or Protestant. I used a similar recruitment strategy and interview guide in the Tutwiler facility as in the Parchman facility. A total of 40 interviews were conducted during a three-month period.

The average age of those interviewed was just under 37, and the racial composition was 50 percent white, 45 percent black, and 5 percent Latina. The mean length of current sentence was about 16 years. The demographics for the study participants mirrored those of the full prison population. Results for the 40 in-depth interviews with women inmates are discussed in Chapters 4, 6, and 8.

## Data Source 4: In-Depth Interviews at a Women's Halfway House

The final data source consists of 70 in-depth interviews at a faith-based halfway house for women in the southern United States (hereafter referred to as the center). In operation since 2002, the center is an outgrowth of the work of a local parishioner who started with a small scripture study group in a women's prison. The parishioner then worked with the state department of corrections to create a transition program for inmates who were within one year of release. the center currently serves about 450 women and children. In addition to inmates still under state supervision, the center also houses women who are there voluntarily because of drug or alcohol problems, domestic abuse, and economic disadvantage.

I worked with staff members at the facility to recruit participants. Specifically, I asked staff members to make announcements during regular religious services and to post notices that volunteers were sought who were willing to discuss their experiences at the facility. Our only stipulations in recruitment were that volunteers should be at least 19 years old (the minimum age for adult status in the state) and have resided at the facility for at least two months. In compliance with Institutional Review Board guidelines, I informed all participants that the interviews would be conducted with a researcher not affiliated with the prison or state department of corrections, would be completely voluntary and confidential, and would not result in any special rewards for participating or punishments for declining participation.

I scheduled interviews with residents who volunteered. All participants received oral and written summaries of the research project and were then asked to sign a consent form. I interviewed a total of 70 residents at the center over the course of a 14-month period. The purpose of the interviews was to investigate how women undergoing difficult life circumstances (including incarceration, drug and alcohol addiction, domestic violence, unemployment, and homelessness) articulate and maintain faith-based identities that allow them to reinterpret their past lives, give meaning to their current lives, and offer hope for the future.

Each interview began with a discussion of the events leading to their admission to the center. Interviewees were then asked to describe the religious and educational programs at the center and how they were able to adjust. In particular they were asked how they had changed since admission to the center and whether the religious programs played a part in that change. Interviewees were then asked to describe the current and previous difficult situations they encountered and whether religion helped them to cope with these situations. Each interview ended with a discussion of the future for each resident. Interviewees were asked about their prospects for the future and what role their faith and the center would play in accomplishing their goals and avoiding further negative situations. Volunteers received $20 upon completion of the interview. This amount was chosen because it was enough to encourage cooperation, but not enough to coerce participation. It is also consistent with previous remunerations in similar types of research (Copes, Brown, and Tewksbury 2011).

The median age for the 70 interviewees was 32.5 and the ages ranged from 19 to 66. The racial/ethnic composition was 55 white women, 14 black women, and 1 American Indian woman, which is consistent with the racial distribution of the center. Forty of the 70 women had at least a high school degree, and nearly half of those had college credits. Sixty percent had worked full- or part-time prior to admission to the center, but the median income was under $10,000.

On average interviewees reported approximately three misdemeanor arrests, two felony arrests, and one felony conviction. Among those arrests, nearly 60 percent were for drug offenses, about 20 percent were for property offenses, and only about 10 percent were for violent offenses. Just over 20 percent of the interviewees were currently or had previously been incarcerated. About 80 percent of interviewees had been physically abused as children or adults, and about 60 percent had been sexually abused. Finally, for religious background, 39 of the 70 women attended church once per week or more as youths. Of those who attended church, nearly all were affiliated with a Protestant congregation, and just over 70 percent attended a Baptist congregation. All but six women reported a conversion or "born again" experience at some point in their lives. This level of exposure to and participation in evangelical Christian religion among interviewees was consistent with the religious background of all residents at the center. Results from the interviews with 70 women at the faith-based halfway house are presented in Chapters 4, 7, and 8.

## Using Semistructured Interviews and Qualitative Data Analysis

The interviews in all four settings were semistructured and free of academic jargon so that participants could speak openly with their own terminology. This is particularly important given the complex nature of personal faith and religious experience, as well as the lack of previous qualitative studies of faith in correctional contexts. As with any qualitative inquiry it was important for us to interview enough individuals to reach "theoretical saturation." Theoretical saturation occurs when "no additional data are being found whereby the [researcher] can develop properties of the category. As he sees similar instances over and over again, the researcher becomes empirically confident that a category is saturated" (Glaser and Strauss 1967, p. 65). It is often difficult at the outset of a research project to determine how many people to interview to reach theoretical saturation. Creswell (1998) recommends 20 to 30 interviews, but Guest, Bunce, and Johnson (2006) concluded that with only 12 interviews, researchers can reach 92 percent saturation for most topics. Given that my research included 63 interviews with men in prison, 40 interviews with women in prison, 30 interviews with prison ministry workers, and 70 interviews with residents of a women's halfway house, I have full confidence that theoretical saturation has been reached and that these 203 narratives are sufficient for elucidating the key topics in this book.

The interviews typically lasted between 45 and 90 minutes and were audio-recorded with permission of each participant. Trained personnel transcribed all interviews and replaced identifying names with aliases. Once all transcriptions were completed in Microsoft Word, the audio files were destroyed. To ensure interrater reliability, I assembled a research team for each project. These teams consisted typically of undergraduate honors students, graduate students, and faculty colleagues (Kerley and Copes 2009; Kerley, Copes, Linn, et al. 2011; Kerley, Copes, Tewksbury, et al. 2011; Kerley et al. 2010; Kerley, Matthews, and Shoemaker 2009). For each data source, team members read each transcript independently to identify common themes. The team then convened to determine the overarching themes identified by all. Initially the relevant, predetermined research issues were broadly coded into "nodes" or categories. This broad coding scheme left a great deal of scope for a more detailed analysis directed toward establishing within-issue variations from one concept to the next. The team carried out this analysis by reading the text for each category and, for each one, creating subcategories that captured distinctions recognized by the participants themselves as important.

### Selection Bias and Generalizability

It is sometimes the case in qualitative inquiry that questions are raised about potential biases among volunteers who agree to be interviewed. The question could be raised whether the self-selection of active religious participants—chaplains, local religious congregants, inmates, or center residents—would yield results that were sanguine for religion. This would be an important issue if the purpose of the book was to determine the efficacy of faith-based programs. Instead, my purpose is to understand the lived experience of faith in correctional contexts. The target population, therefore, is those who have participated in faith-based programs.

As with any qualitative study in which a nonrandom sample is used, care must be exercised to avoid generalizing the results to all inmates, prison ministry workers, and residents of halfway houses. Although I might anticipate somewhat similar results in other states or regions with similar characteristics, additional research is needed to confirm this.

# Bibliography

Acorn, L. 1990. "Correctional Chaplains: The Challenges of Ministering to a Captive Congregation." *Corrections Today* 52, 97–98,106–107.

ADOC (Alabama Department of Corrections). 2010a. http://www.doc.state.al.us /docs/AnnualRpts/2010AnnualReport.pdf.

ADOC (Alabama Department of Corrections). 2010b. http://www.doc.state.al.us /faq.asp#facilities.

ADOC (Alabama Department of Corrections). 2012. http://www.doc.state.al.us /faq.asp#population.

Andrews, D. A., I. Zinger, R. D. Hoge, J. Bonta, P. Gendreau, and F. T. Cullen. 1990. "Does Correctional Treatment Work? A Clinically Relevant and Psychologically Informed Meta-Analysis." *Criminology* 28, 369–404.

Applegate, B. K., F. T. Cullen, B. S. Fisher, and T. Vander Ven. 2000. "Forgiveness and Fundamentalism: Reconsidering the Relationship Between Correctional Attitudes and Religion." *Criminology* 38, 719–754.

Athens, L. A. 1995. "Dramatic Self-Change." *The Sociological Quarterly* 36, 571–586.

Austin, J., and J. Irwin. 2012. *It's About Time: America's Imprisonment Binge*. 4th ed. Belmont, CA: Wadsworth.

Baier, C., and B. R. E. Wright. 2001. "If You Love Me, Keep My Commandments: A Meta-Analysis of the Effect of Religion on Crime." *Journal of Research in Crime and Delinquency* 38, 3–21.

Bartkowski, J. P. 2001. *Remaking the Godly Marriage: Gender Negotiations in Evangelical Families*. Piscataway, NJ: Rutgers University Press.

Bartkowski, J. P. 2004. *The Promise Keepers: Servants, Soldiers, and Godly Men*. Piscataway, NJ: Rutgers University Press.

Bartkowski, J. P., and H. A. Regis. 2003. *Charitable Choices: Religion, Race, and Poverty in the Post-Welfare Era*. New York: New York University Press.

Baylor University. 2005. *The Baylor Religion Survey*. Waco, TX: Baylor Institute for Studies of Religion. http://www.thearda.com/archive/files /descriptions/BRS2005.asp.

Benda, B. B., and R. F. Corwyn. 1997. "Religion and Delinquency: The Relationship After Considering Family and Peer Influences." *Journal for the Scientific Study of Religion* 36, 81–92.

BJS (Bureau of Justice Statistics). 2002. "Recidivism of Prisoners Released in 1994." Technical Report. Washington, DC: US Department of Justice. http://bjs.ojp.usdoj.gov/content/pub/pdf/rpr94.pdf.

BJS (Bureau of Justice Statistics). 2012a. "Correctional Populations in the United States 2011." Technical Report. Washington, DC: US Department of Justice. http://bjs.gov/content/pub/pdf/cpus11.pdf.

BJS (Bureau of Justice Statistics). 2012b. "Prisoners in 2011." Technical Report. Washington, DC: US Department of Justice. http://bjs.ojp.usdoj .gov/content/pub/pdf/p11.pdf.

Blanchard, T. C., J. P. Bartkowski, T. L. Matthews, and K. R. Kerley. 2008. "Religion, Morality, and Mortality: The Ecological Impact of Religion on Population Health." *Social Forces* 86, 1591–1620.

Britt, C. L. 1998. "Race, Religion, and Support for the Death Penalty: A Research Note." *Justice Quarterly* 15, 175–191.

Brock, T. C. 1962. "Implications of Conversion and Magnitude of Cognitive Dissonance." *Journal for the Scientific Study of Religion* 1, 198–203.

Burkett, S. R., and M. White. 1974. "Hellfire and Delinquency: Another Look." *Journal for the Scientific Study of Religion* 13, 455–462.

Camp, S. D., D. M. Daggett, O. K. Kwon, and J. Klein-Saffran. 2008. "The Effect of Faith Program Participation on Prison Misconduct: The Life Connections Program." *Journal of Criminal Justice* 36, 389–395.

Camp, S. D., J. Klein-Saffran, O. K. Kwon, D. M. Daggett, and V. Joseph. 2006. "An Exploration into Participation in a Faith-Based Prison Program." *Criminology and Public Policy* 5, 529–550.

Clear, T. R., Hardyman, P. L., Stout, B., Lucken, K., and H. R. Dammer. 2000. "The Value of Religion in Prison." *Journal of Contemporary Criminal Justice* 16, 53–74.

Clear, T. R., B. D. Stout, H. R. Dammer, L. Kelly, P. L. Hardyman, and C. Shapiro. 1992. "Does Involvement in Religion Help Prisoners Adjust to Prison?" *NCCD Focus* (November), 1–7.

Clear, T. R., and M. T. Sumter. 2002. "Prisoners, Prison, and Religion: Religion and Adjustment to Prison." *Journal of Offender Rehabilitation* 35, 127–159.

Cochran, J. K., and R. L. Akers. 1989. "Beyond Hellfire: An Exploration of the Variable Effects of Religiosity on Adolescent Marijuana and Alcohol Use." *Journal of Research in Crime and Delinquency* 26, 198–225.

Cochran, J. K., P. B. Wood, B. J. Arneklev. 1994. "Is the Religiosity-Delinquency Relationship Spurious? A Test of Arousal and Social Control Theories." *Journal of Research in Crime and Delinquency* 31, 92–123.

Coleman, J. 1988. "Social Capital in the Creation of Human Capital." *American Journal of Sociology* 94, 95–120.

Colson, C. W. 1976. *Born Again*. Grand Rapids, MI: Chosen Books.

Colson, C. W. 1979. *Life Sentence*. New York: Baker Book House.

Copes, H., A. Brown, and R. Tewksbury. 2011. "A Content Analysis of Ethnographic Research Published in Top Criminology and Criminal Justice Journals from 2000–2009." *Journal of Criminal Justice Education* 22, 341–359.

Craig, S. C. 2009. "A Historical Review of Mother and Child Programs for Incarcerated Women." *Prison Journal* 89, 35S–53S.

Creswell, J. 1998. *Qualitative Inquiry and Research Design: Choosing Among Five Traditions*. Thousand Oaks, CA: Sage.

Cullen, F. T., and P. Gendreau. 2001. "From Nothing Works to What Works: Changing Professional Ideology in the 21st Century." *Prison Journal* 27, 313–338.

Curry, T. R. 1996. "Conservative Protestantism and the Perceived Wrongfulness of Crimes." *Criminology* 34, 453–464.

Desmond, S. A., J. T. Ulmer, and C. D. Bader. 2013. "Religion, Self Control, and Substance Abuse." *Deviant Behavior* 34, 384–406.

Dodge, M., and M. R. Pogrebin. 2001. "Collateral Costs of Imprisonment for Women: Complications of Reintegration." *The Prison Journal* 81, 42–54.

Ellis, L. 1987. Religiosity and Criminality from the Perspective of Arousal Theory. *Journal of Research in Crime and Delinquency*, 24, 215–232.

Ellison, C. G. 1991. "Religious Involvement and Subjective Well-Being." *Journal of Health and Social Behavior* 32, 80–99.

Ellison, C. G. 1992. "Are Religious People Nice People? Evidence from the National Survey of Black Americans." *Social Forces* 71, 411–430.

Ellison, C. G., J. D. Boardman, D. R. Williams, and J. J. Jackson. 2001. "Religious Involvement, Stress, and Mental Health: Findings from the 1995 Detroit Study." *Social Forces* 80, 215–249.

Ellison, C. G., and J. S. Levin. 1998. "The Religion-Health Connection: Evidence, Theory, and Future Directions." *Health Education and Behavior* 25, 700–720.

Emerson, M. O., and C. Smith. 2000. *Divided by Faith: Evangelical Religion and the Problem of Race in America*. New York: Oxford University Press.

Gallup. 2010. "Mississippians Go to Church the Most; Vermonters, Least." Technical Report. http://www.gallup.com/poll/125999/mississippians-go-church-most-vermonters-least.aspx.

Gendreau, P., and T. Little. 1996. "A Meta-Analysis of the Predictors of Adult Offender Recidivism: What Works!" *Criminology* 34, 575–608.

Gibbons, D. C. 1999. "Review Essay: Changing Lawbreakers—What Have We Learned Since the 1950s?" *Crime and Delinquency* 45, 272–293.

Giordano, P. 2002. "Gender, Crime, and Desistance: Toward a Theory of Cognitive Transformation." *American Journal of Sociology* 107, 990–1064.

Glaser, B. G., and A. L. Strauss. 1967. *The Discovery of Grounded Theory: Strategies for Qualitative Research*. Chicago, IL: Aldine.

Glaser, D. 1964. *The Effectiveness of a Prison and Parole System*. Indianapolis, IN: Bobbs-Merrill.

Glenmary Research Center. 2000. "Churches and Church Membership Study." Technical Report. http://www.thearda.com/Archive/Files/Descriptions/RCMSST.asp

Grisham, J. 1995. *The Chamber*. New York: Random House Publishing Group.

Guest, G., A. Bunce, and L. Johnson. 2006. "How Many Interviews Are Enough? An Experiment with Data Saturation and Variability." *Field Methods* 18, 59–82.

Harer, M. D., and D. J. Steffensmeier. 1996. "Race and Prison Violence." *Criminology* 34, 323–355.

Harris, A. 2011. "Constructing Clean Dreams: Accounts, Future Selves, and Social and Structural Support as Desistance Work." *Symbolic Interaction* 34, 63–85.

Hassine, V. 1999. *Life Without Parole*. Los Angeles, CA: Roxbury.

Heiney, S. P., J. McWayne, and J. Teas. 2007. "Being Real on Holy Ground: The Lived Experience of Chaplains." *Journal of Psychology and Christianity* 26, 26–32.

Hempel, L. M., and J. P. Bartkowski. 2008. "Scripture, Sin, and Salvation: Theological Conservatism Reconsidered." *Social Forces* 86, 1647–1674.

Hewitt, J. D. 2006. "Having Faith in Faith-Based Prison Programs." *Criminology and Public Policy* 5, 551–558.

Higgins, P. C., and G. L. Albrecht. 1977. "Hellfire and Delinquency Revisited." *Social Forces* 55, 952–958.

Hirschi, T. 1969. *Causes of Delinquency*. Berkeley: University of California Press.

Hirschi, T., and R. Stark. 1969. "Hellfire and Delinquency." *Social Problems* 17, 202–213.

Iannaccone, L. R. 1994. "Why Strict Churches Are Strong." *American Journal of Sociology* 99, 1180–1211.

Ingram, L. C. 1989. "Evangelism as Frame Intrusion: Observations on Witnessing in Public Places." *Journal for the Scientific Study of Religion* 28, 17–26.

Irwin, J. 1985. *The Jail*. Berkeley: University of California Press.

Irwin, J. 2005. *The Warehouse Prison*. Los Angeles, CA: Roxbury Publishing.

James, W. 1902. *The Varieties of Religious Experience: A Study in Human Nature*. New York: Modern Library.

Jiang, S., and T. L. Winfree. 2006. "Social Support, Gender, and Inmate Adjustment to Prison Life." *The Prison Journal* 86, 32–55.

Johnson, B. R. 1987a. "Religiosity and Institutional Deviance: The Impact of Religious Variables upon Inmate Adjustment." *Criminal Justice Review* 12, 21–30.

Johnson, B. R. 1987b. Religious Commitment Within the Corrections Environment: An Empirical Assessment. In J. A. Day and W. S. Laufer (Eds.), *Crime, Values, and Religion* (pp. 193–210). Norwood, NJ: Ablex.

Johnson, B. R. 2002. "Assessing the Impact of Religious Programs and Prison Industry on Recidivism: An Exploratory Study." *Texas Journal of Corrections* 28, 7–11.

Johnson, B. R. 2003. "The InnerChange Freedom Initiative: A Preliminary Evaluation of a Faith-Based Prison Program." Technical Report. Philadelphia, PA: University of Pennsylvania Center for Research on Religion and Urban Civil Society.

Johnson, B. R. 2004. "Religious Programs and Recidivism Among Former Inmates in Prison Fellowship Programs: A Long-Term Follow-up Study." *Justice Quarterly* 21, 329–354.

Johnson, B. R. 2011. *More God, Less Crime: Why Faith Matters and How It Could Matter More*. West Conshohocken, PA: Templeton Press.

Johnson, B. R., S. De Li, D. B. Larson, and M. McCullough. 2000. "A Systematic Review of the Religiosity and Delinquency Literature." *Journal of Contemporary Criminal Justice* 16, 32–52.

Johnson, B. R., and S. J. Jang. 2012. "Crime and Religion: Assessing the Role of the Faith Factor." In R. Rosenfeld, K. Quinet, and C. Garcia (Eds.), *Contemporary Issues in Criminological Theory and Research: The Role of Social Institutions* (pp. 117–149). Belmont, CA: Wadsworth.

Johnson, B. R., S. J. Jang, D. B. Larson, and S. De Li. 2001. "Does Adolescent Religious Commitment Matter? A Reexamination of the Effects of Religiosity on Delinquency." *Journal of Research in Crime and Delinquency* 38, 22–43.

Johnson, B. R., D. B. Larson, S. De Li, and S. J. Jang. 2000. "Escaping From the Crime of Inner Cities: Church Attendance and Religious Salience Among Disadvantaged Youth." *Justice Quarterly* 38, 22–43.

Johnson, B. R., D. B. Larson, and T. C. Pitts. 1997. "Religious Programs, Institutional Adjustment, and Recidivism Among Former Inmates in Prison Fellowship Programs." *Justice Quarterly* 14, 145–165.

Johnson, R., and H. Toch. 1982. *The Pains of Imprisonment.* Prospect Heights, IL: Waveland.

Johnson, P. 1959. *Psychology of Religion.* New York: Abington Press.

Kerley, K. R. 2009. "Religion and Crime." In J. M. Miller (Ed.), *21st Century Criminology: A Reference Handbook* (pp. 144–152). Thousand Oaks, CA: Sage.

Kerley, K. R., M. C. Allison, and R. D. Graham. 2006. "Investigating the Impact of Religiosity on Emotional and Behavioral Coping in Prison." *Journal of Crime and Justice* 29, 71–96.

Kerley, K. R., J. P. Bartkowski, T. L. Matthews, and T. L. Emond. 2010. "From the Sanctuary to the Slammer: Exploring the Narratives of Evangelical Prison Ministry Workers." *Sociological Spectrum* 30, 504–525.

Kerley, K. R., and H. Copes. 2009. "Keepin' My Mind Right": Identity Maintenance and Religious Social Support in the Prison Context." *International Journal of Offender Therapy and Comparative Criminology* 53, 228–244.

Kerley, K. R., H. Copes, A. J. Linn, L. Eason, N. M. Nguyen, and A. M. Stone. 2011. "Understanding Personal Change in a Women's Faith-Based Transitional Center." *Religions* 2, 184–197.

Kerley, K. R., H. Copes, R. Tewksbury, and D. A. Dabney. 2011. "Examining the Relationship Between Religiosity and Self-Control as Predictors of Prison Deviance." *International Journal of Offender Therapy and Comparative Criminology* 55, 1251–1271.

Kerley, K. R., T. L. Matthews, and T. C. Blanchard. 2005. "Religiosity, Religious Participation, and Negative Prison Behaviors." *Journal for the Scientific Study of Religion* 44, 443–457.

Kerley, K. R., Matthews, T. L. and J. Shoemaker. 2009. "A Simple Plan, A Simple Faith: Chaplains and Lay Ministers in Mississippi Prisons." *Review of Religious Research* 51, 87–103.

Kerley, K. R., T. L. Matthews, and J. T. Schulz. 2005. "Participation in Operation Starting Line, Experience of Negative Emotions, and Incidence of Negative Behavior." *International Journal of Offender Therapy and Comparative Criminology* 49, 410–426.

Krause, N., C. G. Ellison, B. A. Shaw, J. P. Marcum, and J. D. Boardman. 2001. "Church-Based Social Support and Religious Coping." *Journal for the Scientific Study of Religion* 40, 637–656.

Kurtz, E. 1979. *Not-God: A History of Alcoholics Anonymous.* Center City, MN: Hazelden.

Levin, J. S., and L. M. Chatters. 1998. Research on Religion and Mental Health: A Review of Empirical Findings and Theoretical Issues. In H. G. Koenig (Ed.), *Handbook of Religion and Mental Health* (pp. 33–50). New York: Academic Press.

Lipton, D. S. 1996. "Prison-Based Therapeutic Communities: Their Success with Drug Abusing Offenders." *National Institute of Justice Journal* (February), 12–20.

MacKenzie, D. L. 1987. "Age and Adjustment to Prison: Interaction with Attitudes and Anxiety." *Criminal Justice and Behavior* 14, 427–447.

MacKenzie, D. L., and L. I. Goodstein. 1985. "Long-Term Incarceration Impacts and Characteristics of Long-Term Offenders." *Criminal Justice and Behavior* 12, 395–414.

MacKenzie, D. L., L. I. Goodstein, and D. C. Blouin 1987. "Personal Control and Prisoner Adjustment: An Empirical Test of a Proposed Model." *Journal of Research in Crime and Delinquency* 24, 49–69.

MacKenzie, D., J. Robinson, and C. Campbell. 1989. "Long-Term Incarceration of Female Offenders—Prison Adjustment and Coping." *Criminal Justice and Behavior* 16, 223–238.

Mahoney, A., and K. I. Pargament. 2004. "Sacred Changes: Spiritual Conversion and Transformation." *Journal of Clinical Psychology* 60, 481–492.

Maruna, S. 2001. *Making Good: How Ex-Convicts Reform and Rebuild Their Lives*. Washington, DC: American Psychological Association.

Maruna, S., L. Wilson, and K. Curran. 2006. "Why God Is Often Found Behind Bars: Prison Conversions and the Crisis of Self-Narrative." *Research in Human Development* 3, 161–184.

Mcintosh, J., and N. McKeganey. 2000. "Addicts' Narratives of Recovery from Drug Use: Constructing a Non-Addict Identity." *Social Science and Medicine* 50, 1501–1510.

MDOC (Mississippi Department of Corrections). 2011. http://www.mdoc.state.ms.us/Research%20and%20Statistics/MDOCBudget/Cost%20Summary-%201992-2011.pdf.

National Center for Education Statistics. 2011. http://nces.ed.gov/programs/stateprofiles/sresult.asp?mode=short&s1=01.

O'Connor, T. P., and N. J. Pallone. (Eds.). 2002. *Religion, the Community, and the Rehabilitation of Criminal Offenders*. New York: Haworth Press.

Olphen, J. V., M. J. Eliason, N. Freudenberg, and M. Barnes. 2009. "Nowhere to Go: How Stigma Limits the Options of Women Drug Users After Release from Jail." *Substance Abuse Treatment, Prevention, and Policy* 4, 1–10.

Operation Starting Line. (2002). Where it all begins in the race against crime. Fact Sheet. Washington, DC: Prison Fellowship Ministries. Also available online at http://operationstartingline.net/channelroot/whatisosl/index.htm.

Oshinsky, D. M. 1997. *Worse Than Slavery: Parchman Farm and the Ordeal of Jim Crow Justice*. New York: Free Press.

Owen, B. 1998. *In the Mix*. Albany: State University of New York Press.

Pargament, K. 1997. *The Psychology of Religion and Coping Theory, Research, Practice*. New York: Guilford Press.

Petersilia, J. 2003. *When Prisoners Come Home: Parole and Prisoner Reentry*. New York: Oxford University Press.

Pew Forum on Religion and Public Life. 2007. "Religious Composition of the U.S." US Religious Landscape Survey. Technical Report. http://www.religionfacts.com/religion_statistics/church_attendance_by_state.htm.

Reed, John Shelton. 1993. *My Tears Spoiled My Aim, and Other Reflections on Southern Culture*. Columbia: University of Missouri Press.

Rhodes, T., S. Bernays, and K. Houmoller. 2010. "Parents Who Use Drugs: Accounting for Damage and Its Limitation." *Social Science and Medicine* 71, 1489–1497.

Richie, B. E. 2001. "Challenges Incarcerated Women Face as They Return to Their Communities: Findings from Life History Interviews." *Crime and Delinquency* 47, 368–389.

Sandifer, J. L. 2008. "Evaluating the Efficacy of a Parenting Program for Incarcerated Mothers." *The Prison Journal* 88, 423–445.

Severance, T. A. 2004. "Concerns and Coping Strategies of Women Inmates Concerning Release: 'It's Going to Take Somebody in My Corner.'" *Journal of Offender Rehabilitation* 38, 73–97.

Severance, T. A. 2005. "'You Know Who You Can Go To': Cooperation and Exchange Between Incarcerated Women." *The Prison Journal* 85, 343–367.

Sherkat, D. E., and C. G. Ellison. 1999. "Recent Developments and Current Controversies in the Sociology of Religion." *Annual Review of Sociology* 25, 363–394.

Shover, N. 1996. *The Great Pretenders*. Boulder, CO: Westview Press.

Silver, E., and J. T. Ulmer. 2012. "Future Selves and Self-Control Motivation." *Deviant Behavior* 33, 699–714.

Smith, C. 2002. *Christian America? What Evangelicals Really Want*. Berkeley: University of California Press.

Snow, D. A., and R. Machalek. 1984. "The Sociology of Conversion." *Annual Review of Sociology* 10, 167–190.

Snyder, Z. K., T. A. Carlo, and M. M. C. Mullins. 2002. "Parenting from Prison: An Examination at a Women's Correctional Facility." *Marriage and Family Review* 32, 33–61.

Spivak, A. L., M. Fukushima, M. S. Kelley, and T. J. Jenson. 2011. "Religiosity, Delinquency, and the Deterrent Effects of Informal Sanctions." *Deviant Behavior* 32, 677–711.

Stanley, G. 1965. "Personality and Attitude Correlates of Religious Conversion." *Journal for the Scientific Study of Religion* 36, 60–63.

Stark, R. 1996. "Religion as Context: Hellfire and Delinquency One More Time." *Sociology of Religion* 57, 163–173.

Stark, R., L. Kent, and D. P. Doyle. 1982. "Religion and Delinquency: The Ecology of a 'Lost' Relationship." *Journal of Research in Crime and Delinquency* 19, 4–24.

Sundt, J. L., and F. T. Cullen. 1998. "The Role of the Contemporary Prison Chaplain." *The Prison Journal* 78, 271–298.

Sundt, J. L., and F. T. Cullen. 2002. "The Correctional Ideology of Prison Chaplains: A National Survey." *Journal of Criminal Justice* 30, 369–385.

Sundt, J. L., H. R. Dammer, and F. T. Cullen. 2002. "The Role of the Prison Chaplain in Rehabilitation." *Journal of Offender Rehabilitation* 35, 59–86.

Sykes, G. 1958. *The Society of Captives*. Princeton, NJ: Princeton University Press.

Taylor, W. B. 1999. *Down on Parchman Farm: The Great Prison in the Mississippi Delta*. Columbus: Ohio State University Press.

Tewksbury, R., and S. C. Collins. 2005. "Prison Chapel Volunteers." *Federal Probation* 69, 26–30.

Tewksbury, R., and D. Dabney. 2004. "Prison Volunteers: Profiles, Motivations, Satisfaction." *Journal of Offender Rehabilitation* 40, 173–183.

Thomas, J., and B. Zaitzow. 2006. "Conning or Conversion? The Role of Religion in Prison Coping." *The Prison Journal* 86, 242–259.

Thumma, S., D. Travis, and W. Bird. 2007. "Megachurches Today: 2005 Summary of Research Findings." Technical Report. Hartford Institute for Religion Research. http://hirr.hartsem.edu/megachurch/megastoday2005 _summaryreport.html.

Tuttle, R. G. 1999. *Can We Talk? Sharing Your Faith in a Pre-Christian World.* New York: Abingdon Press.

Ulmer, J. T., S. A. Desmond, S. J. Jang, and B. R. Johnson. 2012. "Religious Involvement and Dynamics of Marijuana Use: Initiation, Persistence, and Desistence." *Deviant Behavior* 33, 448–468.

Unnever, J. D., and F. T. Cullen. 2006. "Christian Fundamentalism and Support for Capital Punishment." *Journal of Research in Crime and Delinquency* 43, 169–197.

Unnever, J. D., Cullen, F. T., and B. K. Applegate. 2005. "Turning the Other Cheek: Reassessing the Impact of Religion on Punitive Ideology." *Justice Quarterly* 22, 304–338.

Unnever, J. D., F. T. Cullen, and J. P. Bartkowski. 2006. "Images of God and Public Support for Capital Punishment: Does a Close Relationship with a Loving God Matter?" *Criminology* 44, 835–866.

U.S. Bureau of the Census. 2011a. http://quickfacts.census.gov/qfd/states /28000.html

U.S. Bureau of the Census. 2011b. http://quickfacts.census.gov/qfd/states /01000.html

Ward, T., and B. Marshall. 2007. "Narrative Identity and Offender Rehabilitation." *International Journal of Offender Therapy and Comparative Criminology* 51, 279–297.

Warren, J. I., S. Hurt, A. B. Loper, and P. Chauhan. 2004. "Exploring Prison Adjustment among Female Inmates: Issues of Measurement and Prediction." *Criminal Justice and Behavior* 31, 624–645.

Welch, M. R., C. R. Tittle, and H. G. Grasmick. 2006. "Christian Religiosity, Self-Control, and Social Conformity." *Social Forces* 84, 411–430.

Williams, R. H., and S. M. Alexander. 1994. "Religious Rhetoric in American Populism: Civil Religion as Movement Ideology." *Journal for the Scientific Study of Religion* 33, 1–15.

Wilson, J., and M. Musick. 1997. "Who Cares? Toward an Integrated Theory of Volunteer Work." *American Sociological Review* 62, 694–713.

Woodberry, R. D., and C. S. Smith. 1998. "Fundamentalism et al,: Conservative Protestants in America." *Annual Review of Sociology* 24, 25–56.

Wooldredge, J. D. 1999. "Inmate Experiences and Psychological Well-Being." *Criminal Justice and Behavior* 26, 235–250.

Wright, K. N. 1989. "Race and Economic Marginality in Explaining Prison Adjustment." *Journal of Research in Crime and Delinquency* 26, 67–89.

Zinnbauer, B. J., and K. I. Pargament. 1998. "Spiritual Conversion: A Study of Religious Change Among College Students." *Journal for the Scientific Study of Religion* 37, 161–180.

# Index

# About the Book

Kent Kerley explores the issue of religion in prison, offering a rich portrait of religious practices and their impacts.

Kerley shows how offenders of all stripes use faith to adapt and survive in difficult institutional settings. He sheds light on the complex processes of religious conversion, discusses the development of tools for "staying straight" in and after prison, and reveals surprising differences between the experiences of men and women. Moving to the realm of policy, Kerley's analysis illuminates the specific mechanisms by which faith-based prison programming can have a positive impact.

**Kent R. Kerley** is associate professor of justice sciences at the University of Alabama at Birmingham.